Breastfee

Baby Weaning

And

Baby Sleep

Learn How to Nourish Your Baby By Breastfeeding and How to Wean The Baby Off the Breastfeeding While Also Ensuring That Everyone Gets Well-Deserved Sleep

By Laura Nicol

Contents

Thank you for buying this book and I hope that you will find it useful. If you will want to share your thoughts on this book, you can do so by leaving a review on the Amazon page, it helps me out a lot.

How to Breastfeed

New Mother's Guide to Tools, Techniques, Foods and Lifestyle Adjustments for Breasfeeding and Nursing the Baby Successfuly Through Different Stages

By Laura Nicol

Introduction to How to Breastfeed

Getting Going With Breast Feeding

Whenever you hold your child for the initial time in the hospital room, you ought to place his lips on your breast. Although your mature milk hasn't cultivated yet, your breasts are still generating a compound called colostrums that assists to shield your child from infections. If your child has issues locating or remaining on your nipple, you should not stress. Breastfeeding is something that is going to need a great deal of persistence and a great deal of practicing.

Don't expect to be a pro whenever you initially begin, so you should not be reluctant to request recommendations or have a nurse demonstrate to you what you have to do. As soon as you begin, bear in mind that nursing should not hurt. Whenever your child latches on, focus on how your breasts feel. If the latching on hurts, break the suction then attempt once again. You ought to nurse fairly often, as the more you nurse, the quicker your mature milk is going to come in, and more milk you'll generate. Breastfeeding for 9 - 15 minutes per breast 7 - 10 times every day is a perfect target.

Crying is an indication of hunger, which implies you ought to, in fact, feed your child before he begins crying. Throughout an initial couple of days, you might need to wake your child to start breastfeeding, and he might wind up going to sleep throughout the feeding. To make sure that your child is eating as it should, you ought to wake him up if it has actually been 4 hours since the last time he has actually been fed. Comfy Feedings can take 40 minutes or longer, and for that reason, you'll desire a comfortable area. You do not wish to be sitting someplace where you are going to be troubled, as it can make the procedure extremely hard.

Why Should You Breast Feed?

For several years, researchers have actually been looking into the components that make breast milk the best food for babies. They have actually found to this day over 200 substances to combat infection, assist the body immune system in developing, helping with digestion, and helping brain grow - nature made properties that science just can not copy.

The essential long term advantages of breastfeeding consist of the minimized threat of allergic reactions, asthma, weight problems, and some types of childhood cancer. The more that researchers keep on discovering, the better the breast milk looks. Along with making your child much healthier, breastfeeding might additionally make him more intelligent. Lots of research studies have actually shown that breastfed infants have a tendency to be more intelligent than babies who were fed with formula or something else.

Breastfeeding does assist with nutrients, and it helps the brain to develop, which is something every mom ought to consider. The advantages for nursing mothers are just as excellent as they are for the baby. The hormones that are launched throughout breastfeeding are going to suppress blood loss after delivery and are going to aid in diminishing the uterus back to its regular size. Over the long term, the breastfeeding mother is going to have a reduced risk of premenopausal breast cancer, which is the type that strikes prior to the age of 50.

The advantages are going to start to show between 3 and 6 months of breastfeeding. By now, you ought to recognize that breast milk is one power-packed fluid. It provides more for your infant than formula or anything else for that matter. As you start to think about the future of your infant, make a dedication to breastfeed him for as long as you feasibly can.

How is Breast Milk Made

In case you have actually ever been expecting, or in case you are expecting now, you have actually most likely observed an alteration in your bra cups. The physical modifications (tender, swollen breasts) might be among the earliest hints that you have actually become pregnant. Numerous professionals think that the color alteration in the areola might additionally be something to take note of when it pertains to breastfeeding.

The establishing placenta promotes the release of progesterone and estrogen, which are going to, consequently, promote the complicated biological system that assists in making lactation possible. Prior to getting expectant, a mix of milk glands, supportive tissue, and fat comprise the bigger parts of your breast.

The truth is, your freshly swollen breasts have actually been getting ready for your pregnancy ever since you were in your mom's womb! When you were born, your primary milk ducts had actually been formed already. Your mammary glands remained quiet up until you reached adolescence when a surge of estrogen induced them to grow and to swell as well. While pregnant, those glands are going to kick into high gear.

Before your infant shows up, glandular tissue has actually changed the bulk of the fat cells. Each breast might get as much as 1 1/2 pounds heavier than previously! Nestled amongst the glandular tissue and fatty cells is an elaborate system of channels or canals called the milk ducts. The pregnancy hormones are going to induce these ducts to increase in both size and number, with the ducts branching out into tinier canals close to the chest wall called ductules. By the end of every duct is a cluster of tinier sacs called alveoli.

The cluster of alveoli is referred to as a lobule, while a cluster of the lobule is referred to as a lobe. Each breast is going to include approximately 15 - 20 lobes, with one milk duct for every lobe. The milk is generated within the alveoli, which is surrounded by small muscles that squeeze the glands and assist in pressing the milk out into the ductules. Those ductules are going to lead a larger duct that broadens into a milk pool straight beneath the areola.

The milk pools are going to serve as reservoirs that hold the milk up until your child sucks it via the small openings in your nipples. Nature is so clever that your milk duct system is going to end up being completely established about the time of your 2nd trimester, so you can effectively breastfeed your child even if he/she comes in sooner than you are expecting.

Pros Of Breast Feeding

When you have actually delivered, breastfeeding is the single crucial thing you may do to shield your child and aid in promoting health. Most importantly, breastfeeding is totally free. Together with sparing you cash on HMR (Human Milk Replacement), breastfeeding can additionally assist you to keep your medical costs down. Children that are fed with formula get sicker more frequently and more seriously than children that are breastfed, and they additionally have more breathing infections, ear infections, and other issues.

This could be even truer in case your family actually had a history of allergic reactions. When a child is breastfed, the antibodies pass on from the mom to the child, assisting to shield versus allergies and diseases. As the child's system grows, his body is going to start to create its own antibodies, and he'll be more geared up to manage sensitivities of food. Sucking on the breast is going to additionally aid with the growth of jaw alignment and the growth of the cheekbone.

For this reason, there is less of the requirement for pricey orthodontic work when the kid ages. Unlike formula, breast milk is constantly accessible, handy, and at the appropriate temperature level for feeding. Plus, it consists of all of the minerals and vitamins your growing child requires, sparing you a great deal of cash. Breastfeeding additionally has numerous advantages for the mommy too.

The child sucking at the breast is going to induce contractions right after birth, resulting in reduced bleeding for the mommy. Breastfeeding is going to additionally burn calories, so mommy can drop weight much quicker than if she fed her child with a bottle. Breastfeeding is going to additionally produce a unique bond with the mom and the child - which is something formula can not do.

Nursing Space

When you have actually reached the 3rd trimester, you'll most likely begin stocking up on breast pads, nursing bras, and loose button-down shirts for the following months ahead. While preparing to breastfeed, you can additionally develop your private space, a custom-made breastfeeding space for yourself. Your nursing space ought to show your character. If you like a loud, yet welcoming surrounding, you ought to think about being in the corner of the living room.

Keep an additional chair close to you so loved ones, and even buddies can keep you company. If you prefer solitude, a relaxing study or an unfilled guest room would be perfect. You can shut the door, dim the lights down, and after that, take a couple of deep breaths while you breastfeed. Regardless of if it's an overstuffed recliner, glider, or desk chair with wheels, you ought to make certain your nursing chair is extremely comfy. You'll be sitting in the chair for hours every day, so you'll wish it to be extremely comfy.

You ought to constantly search for one that provides shoulder and back support, in addition to armrests. You can utilize a low coffee table, footstool, or a stack of pillows to raise your feet as you breastfeed. In case you bring up your legs to bring your child to your breast, you'll prevent potential backache.

Your neck, arms, back, and feet are going to require as much support as you can offer, so do not think twice about surrounding your body with pillows. In case you lay a pillow throughout your lap for your child to lay on, he'll be extremely comfy and that much nearer to your nipple. For additional convenience, you can even acquire a specifically created nursing pillow that is going to surround your waist. You ought to constantly keep a stand or a little table within arm's length of your breastfeeding chair. What you utilize ought to be large enough to hold a coaster and glass of liquid. Some ladies like to drink through a straw, while others choose to drink from the glass.

You'll additionally wish to keep healthy treats on hand also, like fresh fruit, crackers, or nuts and peanut butter to assist you in changing the energy you utilize while you breastfeed. In case your child has a large appetite or is a slow eater, you might wish to keep yourself occupied while he feeds. You can fill the bookcase or the racks of a close-by cabinet with crossword puzzles or your preferred books to amuse yourself up until your child is full. You ought to additionally keep a phone close by too so that you can speak with friends or family to kill time.

Which Food to Stay Away From While Breast Feeding

Lots of ladies discover that they can eat whatever they like throughout breastfeeding. Despite the fact that it holds true that some highly preferred foods can alter the taste of the milk, numerous infants appear to delight in the varieties of breast milk flavors. Sometimes, Your child might get irritable at the breast after you eat specific foods. If you see this occurring, merely stay away from that specific food. The most typical culprits throughout breastfeeding consist of chocolate, spices, garlic, chili, citrus fruits, gassy veggies, lime, and fruits with laxative impacts, like cherries and prunes.

You can have a cup or 2 of coffee a day, although excessive caffeine can hinder your infant's sleep and even make him/her grouchy. Bear in mind, caffeine is discovered in numerous teas sodas and even nonprescription medication too. It's alright to have a liquor every once in a while, although having more than one beverage can boost your blood alcohol level, placing the alcohol into your breast milk. If you intend to have more than one drink at once, it's ideal to wait 2 hours or more per drink prior to resuming any kind of breastfeeding or nursing.

While breastfeeding, any kind of heavy drinking ought to be stayed away from. Before you, in fact, leave any foods out of your diet plan, you ought to speak to your physician. If you stay away from particular foods and it induces a dietary imbalance, you might have to see a nutritional expert for recommendations on taking other foods or getting dietary supplements.

Selecting A Breast Pump

The milk creation in the breasts, similar to many other things, functions on supply and demand. The more breast milk your infant takes in, the more your body is going to have to create. Breast pumps are usually utilized to guarantee the ongoing creation of breast milk when you can not feed your infant - whether you are back to work, taking a trip, taking medication, or just out of town. Breast pumps can either be battery-powered, manual, semi-automatic electrical or perhaps self cycling electric.

Manual hand pumps are developed to utilize the power of arm muscles or your hand for pumping a single breast at a time. You can additionally get pumps that are going to utilize the foot and leg muscles for pumping both breasts at a single time. Moms with carpal tunnel syndrome might wish to think about utilizing a pump created for leg or arm muscles or perhaps an automated design.

The battery ran pumps with battery are the most ideal for ladies who have an established milk supply and wish to pump one time and even two times a day. These pumps utilize batteries to generate suction, lessening any kind of muscle exhaustion. A lot of battery pumps are created for pumping a single breast at a time and are suggested for periodic use.

Although electrical pumps are more effective than hand and even battery-powered pumps, they additionally have a tendency to be more costly. You can, nevertheless, lease them if you have to. Electric pumps can generally be plugged straight into an outlet and are developed for pumping both breasts at once and even regular usage. Hospital-grade pumps are the most effective for preserving the supply of milk and are obtainable by buying or renting.

How To Utilize A Breast Pump

Much like breastfeeding, pumping is something you learn. When initially having a go at a breast pump, the majority of moms are just able to offer a couple of drops of milk. With the correct practice and understanding, the mom is going to be more effective at pumping.

How to prepare the breast pump:

1. Check out all the guidelines in the kit extremely thoroughly.

2. Every part of the breast pump is going to have to be sanitized prior to utilizing it.

3. After usage, all the parts of the pump are going to have to be cleaned in warm, soapy water, then washed with warm water and drained on a tidy towel. The plastic tubing does not have to be

cleaned up unless you get milk into it. If you do clean it, it ought to be hung to give time to drain and dry completely.

4. If your physician feels the requirement, the whole kit could be sanitized each day.

5. When you initially begin with an electrical pump, the suction level ought to be set on the lowest feasible setting.

Warm compresses, mild nipple stimulation, and mild massages of the breast are going to assist in promoting a fast let down. You ought to constantly unwind while doing breast massages throughout pumping. Some moms choose to close their eyes and then imagine nursing the child, envisioning the child in their arms.

The more unwinded a mom is, the much better let down she'll have, and the more milk is going to be given. Your initial efforts at pumping ought to be taken into consideration as practice while finding out to utilize the breast pump. When you utilize a hand pump, fast, brief pumps at the start are stimulating and are going to mimic more carefully the manner in which a child breastfeeds.

As soon as the let down takes place and milk begins to stream easily, long, steadier strokes are more helpful and less strenuous. When you find out how to pump, you ought to practice for 5 minutes on a side at least one or two times per day. Constantly choose the least demanding part of your day for pumping. Unwinding and recognizing that the pump is your buddy is the single most crucial thing that a mom may do.

There are numerous things that a mom may do to assist herself with unwinding, like putting an image of the child on the pump, playing cards or a game with buddies, seeing tv, reading books, or talking on the phone. Merely seeing the collection bottle is not useful and is going to most likely put excessive tension on you.

First 6 Weeks

Breast milk is the very best food you can offer to your child. Breast milk is a comprehensive food source, consisting of all the nutrients your child requires - a minimum of 400 of them to be precise, consisting of hormones and disease-fighting substances that aren't in a formula. The dietary makeup in breast milk is going to adapt to your child's requirements as he/she grows and establishes. Aside from the brain structure and the infection-fighting advantages of breast milk, which no formula can match, nursing is going to additionally assist in developing a unique bond between your child and you. When nursing, your kid grows on the contact, snuggling, and holding, and the same goes for you.

Because breastfeedings can last up to 40 minutes or more, you ought to select a comfortable area for nursing. The environment is really essential, much more so in the earlier days of breastfeeding when you're still attempting to understand it. If you get quickly sidetracked by sound, go someplace peaceful. You ought to constantly hold your child in a position that will not leave your back or arms aching. It is ideal to support the back of your child's head with your hand, although which position you select depends upon what's more comfy to you.

When supporting your child, a nursing pillow can often be a huge aid. You must never ever feed up until your child, and you are comfy. Take note of how your breasts feel when your child latches on, as his mouth ought to cover the majority of the areola beneath the nipple, and the nipple ought to be in your child's mouth. While some ladies adapt to breastfeeding quickly, other mothers discover it tough to learn. If you feel dissuaded, constantly understand that you aren't the only one.

Breastfeeding is going to take practice. For that reason, you ought to provide yourself as much time as you require to get it down. Constantly take it one feeding at once. In case you are having a terrible day, remind yourself that it'll improve. Bear in mind that any issues are short-lived, as you'll be nursing like an expert by your six-week postpartum examination. The initial 6 weeks are going to be both an experience and training.

You can't hope to understand every little thing when you start, which is where practice and training are going to actually assist you to stand out. The more you breastfeed, the more you'll find out. You'll additionally develop a bond with your child - which is one thing you'll constantly have for the remainder of your lives.

Breast Compression

The sole purpose of breast compression is to carry on the circulation of milk to the child once the child doesn't drink on his own any further. Compressions are going to additionally promote a letdown reflex. This strategy might additionally work for the following:

1. Bad weight gain in the child.

2. Colic in the breastfed child.

3. Regular feedings or lengthy feedings.

4. Aching nipples for the mom.

5. Persistently obstructed ducts

6. Feeding the child who drops off to sleep rapidly.

If every little thing is working out, breast compression might not be required. When all is well, the mom ought to permit the child to finish feeding upon the initial side, and after that, if the child desires more - provide the opposite side.

How to utilize breast compression:

1. Hold the child with a single arm.

2. Hold the breast with another arm, thumb on one side of your breast, your finger on the other far back from the nipple

3. Watch out for the child's drinking, even though there is no requirement to be fanatical about capturing every suck. The child is going to obtain more milk when drinking with an open pause.

4. When the child is munching or drinking no longer, compress the breast, although not so tough that it hurts. With the breast compression, the Child ought to start drinking once again.

5. Maintain the pressure up until the child doesn't drink any further with the compression, then release the pressure. If the child does not stop drawing with the release of compression, wait a little prior to compressing once again.

6. The reason behind releasing the pressure is to enable your hand to rest and to enable the milk to start streaming to the child once again. In case the child stops sucking when you release the pressure, he'll begin once again as soon as he tries the milk.

7. When the child begins to suck once again, he might drink. If not, just compress once again.

8. Carry on feeding on the initial side up until the child doesn't drink anymore and starts to drink on his own.

9. If the child isn't drinking anymore, let it come off the breast or take him off.

10. If the child still desires more, provide the opposite side, and redo the procedure as above.

11. Unless you have aching nipples, you might wish to change sides such as this numerous times.

12. Constantly work to enhance the child's latch.

How to Breastfeed Adopted Babies

Breastfeeding an adopted child is simple, and the odds are that you are going to generate a big quantity of milk. It isn't hard to do, even though it isn't the same as breastfeeding a child you have actually been pregnant with for 9 months.

There are 2 goals that are associated with breastfeeding an adopted child. The initial one is getting your child to breastfeed, and the other is generating ample breast milk. There is more to breastfeeding than simply milk, which is why numerous moms are delighted to feed without hoping to generate milk in the manner the child requires. It's the nearness and the bond breastfeeding supplies that lots of moms search for.

Despite the fact that lots of people feel that the early introduction of bottles might hinder breastfeeding, the early introduction of synthetic nipples can interfere a lot.

The earlier you can get the child to the breast after birth, the much better things are going to be. Children are going to, nevertheless, need the breast so as to remain connected, particularly if they are used to getting circulation from a bottle or some other approach of feeding.

Making Breast Milk

When you have an adopted child, get in touch with a lactation center, and start getting your milk supply prepared. Remember, you might never ever generate a full supply of milk for your child, even though it might take place. Don't ever feel dissuaded by the fact that you might be pumping before the child, as a pump is never ever quite as excellent at drawing out milk as a baby who is properly latched and sucking.

Jaundice

Jaundice is an outcome of the accumulation of bilirubin in the blood that originates from the breakdown of older red cells. It's normal for the red cell to decompose, even though the bilirubin formed does not typically induce jaundice since the liver is going to metabolize it, and after that, eliminate it in the gut.

Nevertheless, the newborn is going to typically end up being jaundiced throughout an initial couple of days because of the liver enzyme that metabolizes the bilirubin ending up being fairly immature. For that reason, newborns are going to have more red blood cells than grownups, and hence more are going to decompose.

There is a condition that's typically called breast milk jaundice, even though nobody understands what, in fact, induces it. So as to diagnose it, the child ought to be at least a week old. The child ought to additionally be fine with breastfeeding alone, having plenty of bowel movements with the passing of clean urine. In this kind of setting, the child has what is called breast milk jaundice.

Occasionally, infections of the urine or an under-functioning of the child's thyroid gland, in addition to other uncommon health problems that might induce the identical kinds of issues, breast milk jaundice is going to peak between 10 and 20 days, even though it can last for 2 - 3 months. In contrast to what you might believe, breast milk jaundice is standard. Hardly ever, if at all, does breastfeeding have to be halted for even a short amount of time. If the child is getting ahead on breast milk, there is no reason whatsoever to quit or to supplement.

Positioning

For some individuals, the procedure of breastfeeding appears to come organically, although there's a degree of capability needed for effective feeding, along with a proper strategy. Inaccurate positioning is among the most prominent explanations for ineffective feeding, and it can even hurt the nipple or breast fairly quickly.

By stroking the child's cheek with the nipple, the child is going to open its mouth towards the nipple, which ought to then be pushed in to ensure that the child is going to obtain a mouthful of nipple and areola. This position is referred to as latching on. Plenty of ladies choose to use a nursing bra to enable simpler access to the breast. The length of feeding time is going to differ.

Despite the period of feeding time, it is essential for moms to be comfy. The following are positions you can utilize:

1. Upright - The sitting posture where the back is upright.

2. Mobile - Mobile is where the mom holds her child in a carrier or a sling while breastfeeding. Doing this enables the mom to breastfeed in daily life.

3. Lying down - This is great for night feeds or for those who have had a cesarean section.

4. On her back - The mom is sitting somewhat upright, additionally a helpful position for tandem breastfeeding.

5. On her side - The mom and child both rest on their sides.

6. Hands and knees - Within this feeding position, the mom is on all fours with the child below her. Remember, this position isn't generally suggested. Anytime you do not feel comfy with a feeding position, constantly stop and change to a separate position. Every position is distinct, while some

moms choose one position; others might like a completely different position. All you need to have to do is to experiment and discover which position is ideal for you.

Breast Feeding Problems

Aching Nipples

Plenty of moms grumble about sensitive nipples that make breastfeeding uncomfortable and discouraging. There is great news, though, as a lot of moms do not suffer that long. The nipples are going to toughen up rapidly and render breastfeeding practically pain-free. Incorrectly located children or infants that suck hard can make the breasts very aching.

Beneath are some methods to alleviate your pain:

1. Ensure your child remains in the proper position considering that a child that isn't placed properly is the top reason for aching nipples.

2. As soon as you have actually finished feeding, expose your breasts to the air, and attempt to shield them from clothes and other irritants.

3. After breastfeeding, administer some ultra-purified, medical-grade lanolin, ensuring to stay clear of petroleum jelly and other items with oil.

4. Clean your nipples with water instead of soap.

5. Lots of ladies discover that teabags ran beneath cold water offer some alleviation when put on the nipples.

6. Make certain that you change your position every time you feed to guarantee that a distinct part of the nipple is being compressed every time.

Blocked Milk Ducts

Blocked milk ducts could be recognized as little, red tender swellings on the tissue of the breast. Blocked ducts can induce the milk to back up and result in infection. The very best approach to unblock these ducts is to make sure that they are as empty as possible. You ought to offer the blocked breast initially at feeding time, and then allow your child to empty it as much as possible. If the milk stays after the feeding, the lingering quantity ought to be gotten rid of by hand or with a pump. You ought to additionally keep pressure off the duct by making certain your bra is not too snug.

Infection

Additionally called mastitis, breast infection is typically because of empty breasts that are out of milk, and bacteria gaining entrance to the milk ducts via fissures or cracks in the nipple, and reduced resistance in the mom because of tension or insufficient nutrition.

The signs of breast infection consist of intense pain or discomfort, the firmness of the breast, soreness of the breast, heat originating from the region, swelling, and even chill. The treatment of breast infection consists of antibiotics, bed rest, increased fluid consumption, painkillers, and administering heat.

Numerous ladies are going to stop breastfeeding throughout an infection, although it's the incorrect thing to do. By clearing the breasts, you'll, in fact, assist in preventing blocked milk ducts. If the discomfort is so bad that you can't feed, attempt utilizing a pump while laying in a tub of warm water with your breasts drifting in the water. You ought to additionally make certain that the pump isn't electrical if you intend to utilize it in the tub.

You ought to constantly make certain that breast infections are dealt with quickly and totally, or you might run the risk of an abscess. An abscess is extremely unpleasant, consisting of throbbing and swelling. You'll additionally experience swelling, ache, and heat in the region of the abscess. If the infection advances this far, your medical professional might recommend medication and even surgical treatment.

Breast Feeding When In Public

Children that are breastfed are extremely portable and simple to comfort regardless of where your schedule has you heading. Lots of ladies nevertheless fret about breastfeeding in public. The concern of nursing in a public location is typically even worse than the real thing, and oftentimes, the only individuals who observe you feeding are the other moms who are doing the identical thing.

Lots of ladies discover methods to breastfeed subtly. You can ask your partner and even a friend to stand ahead of you while you raise your t-shirt from the waist. When you breastfeed, the child's body is going to cover the majority of your upper body, and you can pull your t-shirt to her face to cover the tops of your breast. Some moms choose to place a light blanket around their shoulders as a kind of cover.

When you are going to another person's house, you might feel comfier, either leaving the area or turning away from individuals when you initially place the child to your breast. In case you would like more space, breastfeed in an empty area, vehicle, or public restroom.

Plenty of restrooms are ending up being more baby-friendly, and they even have a different part with a chair and a changing table. Numerous shopping centers now provide special mom's areas where the mother can breastfeed her child in confidentiality. It will not take long before your child is going to find out how to breastfeed with no hassle whatsoever.

An alternative method is pumping your milk in your home, and after that, giving it in a bottle while in public. Bear in mind, using bottles with synthetic nipples in an initial couple of weeks can and most likely is going to hinder breastfeeding.

When breastfeeding in public, you ought to constantly utilize what works ideally for you. Throughout an initial couple of weeks, it is going to take some getting used to, as it is going to be as new for you as it is for the child. After a while, you'll have no issues whatsoever.

In case you do not feel comfy breastfeeding in a specific place, then you should not. You ought to feel a particular level of safety when you feed, as the child can tell when you aren't comfy during something. In case you demonstrate to your child that you aren't worried - you and your child are going to be great.

Toddlers

Since increasingly more ladies are deciding to breastfeed their children, a growing number of them are additionally discovering that they enjoy it enough to continue longer than the first handful of months. Breastfeeding to 3 - 4 years of age prevails in much of the world and is still typical in lots of societies for young children to be breastfed.

Due to the fact that moms and infants typically take pleasure in breastfeeding, you don't have to stop. After 6 months, lots of people believe that breast milk loses its worth - which isn't correct. Even after 6 months, it still has fat, protein, and other essential nutrients which infants and kids require.

The truth is, immune factors in breast milk are going to shield the infant from infections. Breast milk additionally includes things that are going to assist the immune system to develop and other organs to establish and grow too.

It's been revealed and shown in the past that kids in daycare who are still breastfeeding have far less serious infections than the kids that aren't breastfeeding. The mom is going to lose less work time in case she decides to carry on nursing her child once she is back to work.

If you have actually considered breastfeeding your infant as soon as he gets past 6 months of age, you have actually made a smart choice. Although numerous people feel that it isn't needed, breast milk is going to constantly assist infants and young children. Breast milk is the very best milk you can provide to your child.

Regardless of what others might inform you, breastfeeding just has to be stopped when you and the child see eye to eye on it. You do not need to stop when another person desires, you just ought to stop when you feel that it's the correct time.

Engorged Breasts

When you have actually delivered, you might find that your breasts feel puffy, throbbing, sensitive, bumpy, and excessively full. In some cases, the swelling is going to extend completely to your underarm, and you might get a low fever also.

What are the Causes

Within 72 hours of delivering, an abundance of milk is going to come in or end up being accessible to your child. As this occurs, more blood is going to stream to your breasts, and several surrounding tissues are going to swell. As a result, you get swollen, full, engorged breasts.

Not every postpartum mother experienced real engorgement. Some ladies' breasts end up being just a little full, while others discover that their breasts have actually ended up being remarkably hard. Some ladies are going to barely observe the discomfort, as they are involved in other things throughout an initial couple of days.

Treatment

Remember, engorgement is a good indication that you are generating milk to feed to your child. Up until you generate the correct amount:

1. Use a supporting nursing bra, even during the night - making certain it isn't too firm.

2. Breastfeed frequently, every 2 - 3 hours if you can. Attempt to get the initial side of your breasts as smooth as you can. If your child appears pleased with simply one breast, you can provide the other during the following feeding.

3. Stay away from allowing your child to latch on and suck when the areola is extremely firm. To decrease the likelihood of nipple damage, you can utilize a pump up until your areola softens up.

4. Stay clear of pumping milk other than when you have to soften the areola or when your child is not able to latch on. Extreme pumping can cause the overproduction of milk and extended engorgement.

5. To assist with relieving the discomfort and swelling, administer ice bags to your breasts for a brief period of time after you nurse. Squashed ice in a plastic bag is going to work too.

6. Look ahead. You are going to get past this engorgement quickly and shortly be able to delight in your breastfeeding relationship with your brand-new child.

Engorgement is going to pass really rapidly. You can anticipate it to decrease within 1 - 2 days. If you aren't breastfeeding, it is going to usually worsen before it improves. As soon as the engorgement has actually passed, your breasts are going to be softer and still filled with milk.

Throughout this time, you can and ought to continue nursing. Unrelieved engorgement can induce a drop in your generation of milk, so it is essential to breastfeed right from the beginning. Watch for indications of hunger and feed him when he has to be fed.

Diet and Health

The dietary requirements for the child are going to rely entirely on breast milk, and for that reason, the mom is going to have to keep a healthy diet plan. If the child is big and grows quickly, the fat stores acquired by the mom while pregnant could be diminished rapidly, suggesting that she might have a problem eating sufficiently to keep and establish ample quantities of milk.

This kind of diet plan generally consists of a high calorie, high nutrition diet plan which follows on from that in pregnancy. Although moms in starvation conditions can generate milk with dietary material, a mom that is malnourished might generate milk with lacking amounts of vitamins A, D, B12, and B6.

In case they smoke, breastfeeding moms need to utilize exceptional care. More than 20 cigarettes a day have actually been demonstrated to decrease the milk supply and induce vomiting, rapid heart rate, diarrhea, and uneasiness in the babies. SIDS

(Sudden Infant Death Syndrome) is more typical in children that are subjected to smoke.

Heavy drinking is additionally understood to damage the baby, along with yourself. In case you are breastfeeding, you ought to stay clear of alcohol or take in extremely tiny amounts at a time.

The substantial intake of alcohol by the mom can lead to irritation, insomnia, and increased feeding in the baby. Moderate usage, generally 1 - 2 cups a day typically generates no impact. For that reason, moms that are breastfeeding are encouraged to stay clear of caffeine or limit consumption of it.

By following a healthy diet plan and restricting your consumption of the above, you'll guarantee that your child gets the appropriate nutrients throughout your time of breastfeeding. This phase of life is really crucial.

Low Supply Of Breast Milk

Nearly all moms who breastfeed undergo a duration of questioning whether their supply of milk is sufficient. Some moms merely aren't able to generate ample milk to fulfill the requirements of her child. According to lots of professionals, true deficiencies of milk are really uncommon. Plenty of ladies believe that their milk supply is low when it really isn't.

Children that undergo development spurts might desire more milk than typical, and these more regular feedings might leave your breasts short of full. A mom's milk supply might lessen for a short time period if she is not feeding her child frequently enough because of nipple discomfort, or a bad latch method. Diseases and birth control pills might additionally impact the generation of milk.

The very best method to manage a low supply of breast milk is via a physician's care. You ought to make certain that your child gets regular feedings and that absolutely nothing is amiss with your nipples or your milk ducts. Physicians are the very best people to ask, as they are able to run tests to see if every little thing is good inside your body.

A low supply of breast milk can impact your child, even though it's more of a psychological condition than anything else. If your child isn't acquiring any weight or if he is dropping weight, you ought to call a physician instantly. Other strategies for breastfeeding are going to generally assist, even though sometimes weight gain or weight reduction can point to a severe issue. Most of the time, you can still nurse with a short-term reduction in milk supply, even though regular breastfeeding is essential to improving your generation of milk.

Other Foods Aside From Breast Milk

Breast milk is really the only food your child is going to require up until 4 months of age, although the majority of children do well on breast milk alone for 6 months. There is truly no benefit to including other foods or milk before 4 - 6 months unless there are some uncommon conditions.

Water

Breast milk is more than 90% water. Even in the hottest days of summertime, a child will not need any additional water. If a child isn't feeding effectively, they still do not need any additional water - although they are going to have to fix the breastfeeding issues.

Vitamin D

Although breast milk does not consist of much vitamin D, it does have a bit of it. The child is going to accumulate vitamin D throughout pregnancy, and stay healthy with no vitamin D supplements unless you yourself had an issue with vitamin D shortage when pregnant. Direct exposure to the outdoors is going to offer your child vitamin D, even in the winter season. An hour or more of exposure throughout the week is going to provide your child with sufficient vitamin D.

Iron

Breast milk consists of less iron when compared to formulas, specifically those that are iron enriched. Iron is going to provide the child with stronger defense versus infections, as lots of germs require iron in order to multiply. The iron discovered in breast milk is used effectively by the child, while not being accessible to germs. The introduction of iron must never ever be postponed beyond the age of 6 months. Breast milk is the very best that you can feed your child with, as it supplies every little thing he is going to require for most likely the initial 6 months. After the initial 6 months, you can present solid foods to your child in case he is taking a liking to them.

Poor Milk Supply

Nearly all ladies do not have an issue with generating ample milk to breastfeed. The perfect method to make certain that your child is obtaining sufficient milk is to make sure that he's positioned well, and feed him when he's hungry.

Some mothers that are breastfeeding are going to stop before they wish to, merely due to the fact that they do not believe they have ample breast milk. There are indications that may make you think your child isn't obtaining ample milk. If your child appears starving or unsettled after feeding, or if he wishes to feed with brief pauses in between feedings, you might believe he isn't obtaining ample milk, which is often not the case.

There are, nevertheless, 2 trusted indications that let you understand that your child isn't obtaining ample milk. If your child has bad or truly sluggish weight gain or is passing small amounts of concentrated urine, he's not obtaining ample milk. All children are going to drop weight within a couple of days after birth. Babies are born with supplies of fluids, which are going to aid them to keep going for a number of days.

When your child gains back birth weight, he ought to start so. To return to their birth weight, it usually takes a couple of weeks. If the weight gain for your child appears to be sluggish, do not be reluctant to ask your physician or nurse to observe your breastfeeding. In this manner, they can ensure that your method is appropriate and if they believe your child is breastfeeding frequently enough. To assist you with your breastfeeding, here are some manners in which you can boost your supply of milk:

1. Make sure that your child is in a good position and connected to your breast.

2. Allow your child to feed for as long and as frequently as he desires.

3. In case you feel that your child isn't breastfeeding sufficiently, give him more breastfeeds.

4. Throughout each breastfeed, ensure that you offer each breast.

5. If your child has actually been utilizing a dummy, ensure you stop that.

6. Some children might be drowsy and hesitant to feed, which might be the reason behind issues with milk supply.

By following the above pointers, you'll do your part in ensuring you have ample milk when it arrives time to breastfeed. If you are unsure or have other questions, make sure to ask your physician, as he can address any kind of question you might have.

Refusing To Breast Feed

In some cases, a child that is breastfed might unexpectedly choose not to breastfeed. The child is going to retreat from the breast, and after that, toss his head back and forth. This can occur at any time. Refusal to feed on the breast might take place when the child is in pain. Usually, this could be because of the aching head from vacuum delivery, a nearby infection, thrush in the child's mouth, or teething.

Making use of dummies, nipple guards, or teats might additionally add to refusal. Some children discover it really hard to feed upon the breast and bottle as the sucking action is really distinct. Some end up being baffled, and for that reason, you should stay away from utilizing any kind of dummies or teas. In some cases, the milk simply takes bitter. This could be because of antibiotics in case you are at the beginning or at the middle of your period, or nipple creams. In case the milk tastes bitter, your child is usually not going to not want to feed.

You ought to attempt to determine what might have triggered the breast refusal in order to deal with the cause. Constantly stay patient and mild with your child. Make sure you hold your child beside you to ensure that he can take the breast when he wishes to, to ensure that he starts to recognize that breastfeeding is both satisfying and comfy. Older children might unexpectedly take shorter and less frequent breastfeeding sessions, although this can be the case with some babies. It's constantly advised not to attempt to make the child feed longer, but rather to allow the child to choose how frequently and additionally for how long each particular feeding is going to last.

Going Back to Work

When you go back to work, you can keep on breastfeeding. In case you reside near work or have on-site daycare, you might have the ability to breastfeed throughout your breaks. In case that isn't achievable, you have 2 choices:

1. Keep your milk supply by utilizing a top-quality automated electrical breast pump throughout the day. Spare the milk that you gather for your babysitter.

2. In case you do not wish to or can't pump at work, you can slowly substitute daytime feedings with formula while you're at home while still nursing during the night and in the early morning. The milk your body generates might not suffice to keep your child pleased, even in case you just require enough for 2 feedings.

Pros of pumping at work

Pumping at work is going to assist with promoting your generation of milk, so you'll have lots available when it comes time to feed. You can additionally gather the milk you pump, so your child is going to have the dietary and health advantages of breast milk even when you aren't there. To make things better, pumping may be a perfect method to sense a link to your child throughout the workday. Although it can look like an inconvenience, numerous moms discover that the advantages of breast pumping far out weight the trouble.

To handle pumping at work, you'll have to have the following:

1. Breast pump, ideally a completely automated electrical pump with a double collection kit so you can pump both breasts at once.

2. Bags and bottles for gathering and keeping the milk.

3. Access to cooler or fridge to keep the milk cold up until you come home.

4. Breast pads to assist with shielding your clothing in case you begin leaking.

Make certain that you get used to pumping prior to getting back to work, so you'll understand what to anticipate and how it feels. You'll be far more self-assured with pumping at work in case you understand that you can generate ample milk.

At work, you'll wish to have someplace that's far from everybody else when you pump, like an empty room or an empty office. In this manner, you'll be far from everybody else, and you can have the peace you require to pump. In the majority of workplaces, this should not be an issue.

For the time frame, you'll wish to pump every 2 - 3 hours if you can. If you can't, every 4 hours is going to need to be enough. After you have actually wrapped up pumping, keep the milk in the bottles or bags, tidy yourself up, and then return to work.

When you come back home, you can feed the milk to your growing child.

Introducing Solid Foods

Breast milk is all your child is going to require up until it is at least 4 months old. There does arrive a time when breast milk is not going to provide all of your child's nutrition requirements anymore. Full-term babies are going to begin to need iron from other sources when they are 6 - 9 months old.

Some children that don't get going with solid foods by the age of 9 - 12 months might have a terrific level of trouble accepting solid foods. It's really a developmental turning point when your kid begins with solid foods, as he is now maturing.

When to begin, the perfect time to start solid foods is when the child demonstrates interest. Some children are going to demonstrate an interest in solid food when it's on the plate of their parents, as early as 4 months of age. By 5 - 6 months of age, the majority of children are going to reach out and attempt to get the food. When the child begins to grab food, it's typically the time to proceed and provide him with some.

Often, it might be a much better idea to get started with food earlier. When a child appears to get hungry or as soon as weight gain isn't continuing at the preferred rate, it might be great to get going with solid foods as early as 3 months. It might be achievable, nevertheless, to continue breastfeeding alone so that the child is less hungry or developing more quickly.

Breastfed children are going to digest solid foods much better and sooner than synthetically fed children due to the fact that breast milk is going to have enzymes that assist in digesting proteins, fats, and starch. Breastfed children are going to additionally experience a range of distinct tastes in their life, considering that the tastes of numerous foods the mom eats are going to enter her milk.

When the child starts to take in solid foods at the age of 5 - 6 months, there is extremely little distinction in what he begins with or what order it is presented in. You ought to, nevertheless, stay clear of spicy foods or extremely allergenic foods initially, although if your child grabs the potato on your plate, you ought to allow him to have it if it isn't too hot.

Offer your child the foods that he appears to be curious about. Enable your child to take pleasure in the food and do not fret excessively about just how much he takes initially, as much of it might wind up on the ground or in his hair anyways.

The simplest method to obtain iron for your child at 5 - 6 months of age is by offering him meat. Cereal for babies has iron, although it is absorbed poorly and might induce your child to get constipated.

Weaning

When your child has actually stopped breastfeeding and obtains all of his nutrition from the breast, he's, in fact, weaned. Despite the fact that children are additionally weaned from the bottle too, the term weaning typically describes when a child is prevented from breastfeeding.

When weaning is a mom's idea, it typically needs a great deal of persistence and can require time, depending upon the age of your child, and additionally how well your kid adapts. The experience is distinct for everybody.

Weaning is a long farewell, in some cases psychological, and in some cases, unpleasant. It does not nevertheless; signify the end to the intimacy you and your kid have actually established throughout the nursing phase. What it implies is that you need to substitute breastfeeding with other kinds of sustenance.

Getting Started With weaning

You are the very best judge regarding when it's the correct time to wean, and you do not truly have a due date unless you and your kid are, in fact, prepared to wean. The suggested time for weaning is one year. Regardless of what family members, buddies, and even total strangers inform you, there is no correct or incorrect time for weaning.

How Do You Wean?

You ought to carry on gradually, no matter what the age of your kid might be. Specialists claim that you should not withhold your breast abruptly, as the outcomes could be distressing. You ought to, nevertheless, attempt these techniques:

1. Skip a feeding - Skip a feeding and see what occurs, providing a cup of milk to your child rather. Alternatively, you can utilize a bottle of your own pumped milk, cow's milk, or a formula. If you lower feedings one by one, your kid is going to ultimately get used to the modifications.

2. Reduce feeding time - You can begin by reducing the length of time your kid is really at the breast. If the regular feeding time is 5 minutes, attempt 4.

3. Depending upon the age, follow the feeding with a healthy treat. Bedtime feedings are normally the toughest to wean, as they are generally the final to go.

4. Delay and divert - You can delay feedings if you are just feeding a number of times each day. This approach works excellent in case you have an older kid you can, in fact, reason with. If your kid desires the breast, state that you'll feed later on, and then divert him.

If you have actually attempted every little thing and weaning does not appear to be working at all, perhaps he time simply isn't appropriate. You can wait simply a tad longer to see what occurs as your kid and you need to figure out the correct time to wean together.

Baby Weaning

Parent's Guide to Successfully Weaning Their Baby Towards Solid Foods and Raising a Healthy, Happy and Self-Assured Child

By Laura Nicol

Introduction to Baby Weaning

Chapter 1: When Should You Wean Your Baby

When should you wean your baby? There are several theories on this, and it can be among the most frequently asked questions to a pediatrician. Even they might not have the ability to tell you when the procedure ought to be started. The truth is, numerous moms require a clear answer that tells them when they ought to simply stop. One such answer doesn't exist. The truth is, it takes a good deal of time to make this baby weaning procedure occur, and nobody can tell you when to stop breastfeeding.

In the USA, it is approximated that just about 20 percent of babies are still nursing at 6 months of age. This is an extremely low number. When you compare this to most other countries, you might discover that the distinctions are rather striking. For instance, in many European, Asian and African cultures, babies are going to breastfeed up until they are between 2 and 4 years of age. A number of moms in these nations would see stopping breastfeeding so young, as is done in the USA by the majority of moms, as really wrong.

Why should you keep going, or why should you stop? There's no proof that there is any damage to a kid that is breastfed longer. There are lots of advantages to breastfeeding longer. You are going to discover that the kid is obtaining the nutrition it requires. You are going to additionally see that even if you breastfeed your kid simply one time a day, there is an advantage in this. Culturally, individuals in the USA have actually put a black mark on the procedure of breastfeeding past a couple of months; however, this does not need to be the case.

As a parent, remember why you decided to breastfeed, to begin with. The nutrition is perfect for the kid. The bond that forms in between you and the baby is extremely strong. Most significantly, you have actually established a kid that has come to view breastfeeding as a procedure that keeps them comfy and safe.

The procedure of baby weaning is one that has no time restriction. Consider what is right for your kid independently instead of searching for a goal beyond this. Eventually, you ought to motivate your kid to decide by seeing what he/she requires instead of listening to what your friend has actually told you is suitable for them.

Chapter 2: Baby Weaning Resources

When it pertains to weaning a baby from breastfeeding, everybody has a viewpoint. You are going to discover women with no experience providing recommendations on the length of time a baby ought to breastfeed. You might even discover that everybody you know has a distinct opinion regarding when the baby ought to stop breastfeeding. While this prevails, it is necessary to keep in mind that it is extremely crucial to make this decision on your own, based upon what you and your baby require from the procedure. Nevertheless, where can you go for help?

First off, among the very best places to get assistance from is your pediatrician. Your pediatrician ought to be somebody that you trust with your kid's health, and if you do not, you ought to be trying to find another professional to assist you. The truth is, you want to have an excellent idea of what your kid requires at this moment in time, no matter how old they are. Talk with your medical professional about your kid and breastfeeding. Because babies do see their physicians frequently, this is a concern you can discuss whenever you feel it is suitable. The American Academy of Paediatrics advises that babies are breastfed up until they are at least one year of age. However, that does not indicate your medical professional is going to suggest this.

Besides your pediatrician, who understands the health and well being of your kid, there are numerous other locations to get information and guidance on breastfeeding. You might want to keep away from those who might not have a viewpoint that is based upon facts. For instance, in case a friend who has actually never ever breastfed has an opinion, it is not originating from experience. Stay clear of these and speak with somebody that has actually breastfed and learn how they resolved the procedure. You can discover a range of excellent support groups available online, too. This can be a wonderful resource for moms who desire impartial viewpoints on when they ought to think about baby weaning. Remember that it is still your decision to make.

Baby weaning is a procedure that is not simply specified by when you ought to stop breastfeeding, yet additionally by how to do so. You are going to discover the procedure more satisfying after you have actually collected facts and information from trustworthy sources.

Chapter 3: 3 Baby Weaning Misconceptions

Baby weaning is a procedure in which a kid stops breastfeeding from their mom and moves to consuming nothing but solid foods or a from a bottle. This procedure is eventual, and there is no set time table for when it ought to occur. This is particularly true because the majority of babies need to make up their minds by themselves. Each is distinct. Their requirements, both physically and mentally, are different. Because breastfeeding is a lot more than feedings, it is very important to think about all sides of the procedure. When it concerns baby weaning, there are typically numerous misconceptions. Here are 3 to remember.

1: 6 Months Is the Time

Among the worst mistakes you can make is to presume that your kid needs to be weaned by the time they are 6 months old. Actually, the American Academy of Paediatrics advises that moms continue to breastfeed their kids up until at least the age of one. Worldwide, stopping breastfeeding prior to a kid's 2nd birthday is weird. It is actually a decision that the kid has to make. Are they prepared for the shift? If not, they are going to let you know. It is difficult to push a kid just like that.

2: Breastfeeding Lasts Too Long

The truth is, there is no reason to stop breastfeeding early. Numerous kids wish to continue with breastfeeding for one reason or another and ought to be permitted to do so. They ought to be put onto solid foods by the age of 6 months, however, they can supplement this with breastfeeding for a few more years without an issue. Breast milk is extremely healthy throughout a kid's initial years. It can assist to shield their immune system and permits the body to develop appropriately.

3: Weaning Is Too Tough

The procedure of weaning a kid from the breast is one that does require time. The quantity of time it takes actually depends upon the kid. If a kid hesitates to stop breastfeeding, there is likely a reason why this is occurring. In this case, talk with the kid's pediatrician and make sure to work with the kid to comprehend why.

In numerous circumstances, individuals have a mistaken belief about why moms pick to breastfeed for longer than one year. The bottom line is that there is absolutely nothing amiss with the procedure. It does not impact the growth of a kid adversely but does promote a strong immune system.

Chapter 4: Start Baby Weaning

You have chosen that your kid has to be weaned. Now what? There are various techniques for weaning your baby off of breast milk. You can consider all of them as feasible choices, so long as they do work for you. Not everything is going to work, however. The first thing you want to do is to make certain your kid is prepared. To do this, ensure they are old enough and getting sufficient calories from the food they are ingesting. If so, consider these 3 techniques.

1: Skipping A Feeding

Possibly the easiest of techniques is just skipping a feeding. Simply do not do breastfeeding and see how your kid responds. As an alternative to breastfeeding, provide a cup of breast milk or formula. This is maybe among the very best methods because you are just going to carry out a feeding once every week or so. Over the next couple of weeks, not just is the kid going to adjust to this, the body will adjust too.

2: Older Kids Can Postpone

If your kid is old enough to talk with, divert them during the times when you would usually breastfeed them. Rather than really going to sit and breastfeed, take the kid outside for a walk at that time. By doing this, the kid has something to take up his time. If the kid does request breastfeeding, let them know you are going to do that later on. Distract them from it.

3: Shorten the Time

The last technique of weaning enables the breastfeeding mom to shorten the quantity of time that the kid is nursing. Make certain the kid is obtaining all of the food he/she requires from another source, like a healthy treat. Then, gradually cut down on the quantity of time they are breastfeeding. Go from 5 minutes to 3 minutes, down to 2, and so forth. Feedings ought to dwindle. If you are doing this with a kid that is under 6 months of age, it is necessary to change to a bottle-feeding schedule to ensure that no nutrients are lacking.

These 3 approaches are just 3 choices. There are a lot of other techniques out there, too. The objective you ought to have is weaning your baby gradually so that there is no abrupt stopping, which can impact them mentally. When you achieve this, you and the kid are going to be on a course to enhance their capability to stop breastfeeding and your capability to stop fretting about it.

Chapter 5: Tips To Make Weaning Easier

The weaning procedure could be challenging, and it can frequently leave both mom and kid wanting a couple more months (or longer) of the procedure. When the time has actually come to wean your kid from breastfeeding, it could be fantastic. If you put in the time to make it a great step in the appropriate direction, everybody is going to gain from it. Here are some pointers to assist you in making weaning simpler.

1. When you would generally be nursing, introduce your kid to something that is enjoyable or brand-new to them. Even better, take them outside to play throughout this time. They are not even going to consider breastfeeding if you occupy them enough throughout this time.

2. Do not wear the clothes that you generally put on while nursing. This keeps the breastfeeding signal away from the mind. Rather than sitting in your regular nursing area, select other locations in the room to sit. Once again, it busts the connection.

3. For kids that are under a year old, you are going to likely be substituting a breastfeeding session with a bottle or often a cup. Do so when you would usually be feeding the kid. This permits the kid to associate the procedure of breastfeeding with the bottle.

4. For kids that are older than one year, you are going to want to be a bit more imaginative in selecting something to fill this time. Rather than breastfeeding, encourage a healthy treat. Alternatively, you might wish to skip the food entirely and simply plan some time to snuggle together.

5. Ensure there are diversions when typical breastfeeding times are. Daddy can assist here. Encourage daddy to hang around doing something exciting with the kid throughout this time.

6. Do not wean them while they are teething or whenever there is another change taking place in their lives. You do not wish for them to be mentally scarred by the occasion! Let them adjust to other

changes initially, and then present the weaning procedure.

7. Notice that your kid might get another calming habit, like sucking a thumb or hanging on to a blanket. This ought to be fine and not dissuaded because they are merely trying to find security from it. Let them make a psychological break like this.

Promoting breastfeeding throughout any of these circumstances should not be done. By taking these actions, you can securely assist your kid in shifting far from breastfeeding.

Chapter 6: Allowing Your Kid to Naturally Wean

The American Academy of Paediatrics suggests that infants are not pushed to wean at all. They additionally advise that a mom breastfeeds for at least a complete year. The World Health Organization has a distinct view. They encourage kids to breastfeed up until they are 2 years of age. Still, there is no limitation to when you need to stop, and there is definitely no reason to do so prior to the kid being prepared to do so. You ought to enable your kid to wean off breastfeeding when it is natural for them to do so.

Let your kid decide when to breastfeed. Many babies are going to stop breastfeeding between the ages of 12 months and 18 months; however, others might take a bit longer to be prepared to do so. What are a few of the advantages of this natural process? Keep these in mind.

- If the baby graduates to more solid foods and is alright with missing their breastfeeding session, let it be. This reveals that they are self-assured and no longer require the security of your breast to let the procedure of feeding take place.

- Enable your kid to breastfeed longer, and you can skip the bottle requirement completely. Numerous kids go from breastfeeding straight to drinking fluids out of a cup. They do not have to spend plenty of nights struggling with a bottle then. You get to skip the expense of the bottles too.

- Allow the kid to figure out when to stop breastfeeding, and you will not need to go through the withdrawal of the procedure. As they naturally substitute their meals from the breast with meals from the table, they are going to get used to the procedure. So are you. Numerous moms struggle with this procedure due to the fact that it could be extremely confining to understand that your kid is no longer breastfeeding.

Take the procedure one action at a time. They might be piqued by a brand-new taste for breakfast and might feel much better about eating what their brother or sister is. The majority of kids can breastfeed well past the age of one without an issue.

When you let them stop breastfeeding naturally, you both come out as winners. They stay away from much of the risks kids who are fed face. Plus, they are more comfy with the shift if they are part of the move to stop breastfeeding. You might discover that this allows you to be more happy to stop, too.

Chapter 7: Which Age Is Too Old For Breastfeeding?

There are numerous views on the subject of breastfeeding in regards to when you ought to stop it. Eventually, this is a choice that ought to be made by you and your kid, however, there comes a time when every kid needs to make that break from breastfeeding and begin concentrating on a more adult-based diet plan. The concern is when. There are numerous things to remember when enabling your kid to keep breastfeeding beyond the age of one. In the USA, this is taken into consideration as regular, however, in many other nations, kids up to the age of 4 are going to breastfeed. Keeping this in mind, you are going to want to create some strategies and changes.

What To Do

If your kid is not yet all set to stop breastfeeding, there is no reason to stop them from doing so, presuming they are under the age of 4. Throughout this time, however, you are going to wish to move far from the consistent breastfeeding and utilize it more as an occasional reward. It is vital to bear in mind that a kid at the age of 6 months ought to be beginning to consume solid food. Healthwise, they have to be taking in solid food in stages beginning at 6 months. After this time, the majority of their calories ought to be originating from their food, not from breastfeeding. This additionally permits them not to require to nurse to sustain themselves continuously.

Throughout this time, it can additionally be suitable to provide your kid with breast milk. They do not have to breastfeed to get this milk, however. You can put it in their cereal and other foods. They can additionally consume it in a cup. It is suitable to do this up through preschool, in case you feel it is necessary to do so. They must not be dependant on breast milk for calories, though.

Ultimately, you are going to want to make the break from breastfeeding absolutely. It is frequently essential to bear in mind that kids can breastfeed too long. Those that do might have a greater hesitation to stop. Instead of permitting this, a mom has to make certain that the kid is mentally steady and entirely well-fed beyond breastfeeding. Make certain to speak with your pediatrician if you feel that your kid is having a problem with any facet of weaning or if you are uncertain how to approach the procedure with your kid.

Chapter 8: Adding Cuddle Time

Baby weaning is the procedure of making it possible for a baby to stop breastfeeding and instead to work towards consuming either from a bottle, if the kid is younger, or drinking from a cup and consuming solid foods. The time frame for performing this is actually up to the mom and the kid as natural baby weaning ought to constantly be the parent's objective. Yet, when the time comes to begin working towards weaning, you might wish to think about why the kid is resisting. It might be that they are hungry, which indicates changing their meals to include more calories. For lots of other kids, the requirement to breastfeed is not about eating, it is about time together with mommy.

There is a great deal of bonding that takes place between a mom and her kid throughout the breastfeeding experience. This bond is what makes it possible for the kid to be comfy and feel protected as it is young and growing. Ultimately, there is going to come a time when the kid has to stop breastfeeding, however, an issue can occur where the kid is less happy to do so since they yearn for and, in fact, require this intimate time with their parents. The bright side is that you can aid them through this procedure effectively.

It is essential to think about baby weaning with regard to psychological strength. Urging babies to wean typically indicates still providing that close bonding time they require. Only mommy is going to do in numerous circumstances, however, daddy ought to feel like part of the procedure as well. For instance, given that the kid requires that close proximity, it might be an excellent idea to devote some time every day to snuggling instead of nursing. For instance, maybe your kid nurses every day at 11 am. You have actually fed them solid foods, and you are now sitting down to spend some time enjoying a favorite tv program. Snuggle with them at this time. They have a full stomach and simply require the sensation of security that typically accompanies breastfeeding. With some snuggle time, however, they can stop breastfeeding without losing that required security.

As you can see, the procedure of breastfeeding is one that integrates a vast array of various things. You are going to want to satisfy the kid's physical requirements of consuming ample calories. However, you additionally need to think about the kid's requirement for security and comfort. When you can satisfy both of these requirements, everybody involved is going to be in a better place.

Chapter 9: One Meal At A Time

There are lots of methods to encourage baby weaning to occur. There comes a time when you have to make the initial move, however. If it is time to think about baby weaning, you might wish to do the procedure one action at a time. More properly, you wish to do the procedure one meal at a time. Doing so can assist you and your kid to do properly in regard to handling the procedure. If you are prepared to begin weaning, think about the one meal at a time technique to help with that.

Choose A Meal

The initial step is to select a particular meal to start with. Pick a meal you are most comfy with quitting initially. There is no particular requirement regarding what meal to work with. The objective is simply to pick one that works ideally for you. As soon as you understand which one it is going to be, stop breastfeeding at this meal. Rather, add in a healthy solid food meal for the kid. Depending upon the age of the kid, you might want to overcome the steps of offering a baby solid food consisting of selecting cereals initially, and after that, veggies and fruits, etc. If the kid is currently consuming solid foods, you are going to simply substitute one of his/her meals at the breast with solid foods.

Next Up

Keep this up for at least a week. You do not wish to cut the kid off from breastfeeding too rapidly as this can induce the kid to deal with a variety of different sensations, consisting of psychological loss. Rather, every day for the next week, feed the kid that identical meal in solid foods. Do not sit in the identical area you have actually sat for breastfeeding, too

When this has actually been successful for a complete week, you can make the shift to the next meal. Choose the next regular breastfeeding and skip it by substituting it with a healthier meal for the kid. Once again, it does not matter which meal it is, as much as it matters how you go through the procedure. You are just substituting the 2nd meal at the breast with a meal at the table.

Continue to do this, permitting a complete week between each shift. You are going to discover some resistance along the way, however, in many cases, the procedure is going to be successful. Go slowly and work at a rate proper for you and baby.

Chapter 10: Extended Breastfeeding Advantages

For those moms who are not sure of whether they ought to go through the procedure of baby weaning just yet, think about a few of the advantages of prolonged breastfeeding, or breastfeeding your kid past the age of 6 months. Keep in mind to keep an open mind when it pertains to thinking about when you ought to wean your baby from breastfeeding. It ought to be a choice left up to your baby when he/she is lastly comfy to let go of breastfeeding and prefers all solid foods instead.

While not all moms have to utilize prolonged breastfeeding, for some, it looks like what the kid desires. There is absolutely nothing bad about feeding your kid by breast longer than what is considered average. Rather, think about a few of the advantages of the procedure.

1. Breastfeeding offers your baby the advantages that extend to the immune system. To put it simply, they get the immunological benefits that naturally originate from drinking human-made milk. As a kid

is simply a couple of months old, this advantage can help them to stay healthy longer and to fight off a lot of the infections kids get. Toddlers are healthier in case they breastfeed longer.

2. Lots of babies feel that breastfeeding is more than a source of food. It is additionally the location to go when they require comfort from mommy. When they are afraid, dismayed about something, or just hurt, this is among the very best methods to assist the kid in boosting their feelings.

3. You stay clear of much of the typical problems related to non-human milk, particularly allergy symptoms. Lots of kids can additionally gain from the rewards of lower cancer risk from breastfeeding for a longer period of time.

Possibly the greatest advantage to extended breastfeeding is merely helping the kid with deciding on his own. There are a great deal of misunderstandings about the procedure, such as the one that claims the kid is going to end up being too connected to his mom if he breastfeeds for too long. This is just not the case. Rather, the kid is most likely to be healthier and have a more powerful bond with their parents. Additionally, they get assistance when it comes to deciding to stop, and they are mentally and physically prepared to do so.

Prolonged breastfeeding is a choice for a lot of parents. There are few, if any, reasons to quit breastfeeding your kid sooner. Actually, you might discover that it is a lot more appropriate to keep at the procedure for a bit longer.

Chapter 11: How to Get Started

Are you prepared to quit breastfeeding your kid? If so, you might be uncertain of where to begin to quit the procedure. Each kid is distinct, and it is extremely crucial for a parent to make the appropriate decision for their kid. To achieve this, it is really crucial to take into consideration if your kid is ready. Here are some actions to follow to assist you through baby weaning.

Action 1: Identify If Your Kid Is Ready

A kid under the age of 6 months ought to change to a formula if they are not breastfeeding anymore. A kid that is over 6 months ought to be consuming some solid food. Once they are consuming the majority of their calories from solid food, you can think about switching them to a cup rather than breastfeeding.

Action 2: Maintain Security

As you quit breastfeeding, bear in mind that your kid still requires a great deal of security. Every week, get rid of one breastfeeding from the schedule. Throughout that time, do things that keep the kid occupied, yet additionally safe and secure and comfy. Snuggle together. Hang out playing together. This keeps them mentally strong through the occasion. Make certain that the kid has the ability to let go in this way.

Action 3: Maintain Positivity

Each kid is different when it comes to stopping with feeding on the breast. Some are going to ask for it. Others are never going to hesitate about it. It is best to keep the kid who is asking occupied, so there is no worry about the procedure. In case they ask for it, tell them they can breastfeed later on. At the moment, you ought to have something exciting for them to do, like going outdoors to play.

Step 4: Urge Daddy To Get Involved

Now is a good time for daddy to begin assisting with meals and to begin having fun with the baby throughout breastfeeding times. It is frequently essential for daddy to get involved in feeding the kid solid foods so that they can break from believing that just mommy supplies this.

Step 5: Know That Nights Are Hardest

Night breastfeeding, like that before bed, is frequently the toughest time to break from. Encourage the kid to read or simply spend time snuggling together. Have a bedtime treat initially.

The procedure ought to be steady. Motivate your kid to breastfeed if it is required. However, work towards breaking the habit gradually. You and your kid are going to value the procedure if you go through it this way.

Chapter 12: Handling Other People's Advice

Numerous families are going to have a couple of individuals within them that motivate a breastfeeding mom to quit breastfeeding. For some reason, they think that the procedure ought to stop a lot sooner, and because you are the kid's mom, you are not delighted about their remarks. Besides, don't you know what is ideal for your kid? Lots of households have this kind of occurrence. If you are a breastfeeding mommy, it can aid to have some information and pointers to handle those who tell you to quit breastfeeding.

- The American Academy of Paediatricians suggests that kids should be breastfed at least up until they are one year old. There is neither reason nor advantage to quitting before this.

- The World Health Organization urges moms to breastfeed their kids up until the age of 2 years of age. In fact, in numerous nations throughout Europe, Asia, and Africa, kids are breastfed up until they are between the ages of 2 and 4 years of age.

- There is no proof that a kid that is breastfed is any less capable of growing. In fact, kids who get the nutrients from breastfeeding, in fact, grow much better and are less vulnerable to disease consisting of all the things from infections to cancer.

- Babies ought to be motivated to quit breastfeeding just when they are prepared o do so. You ought to not feel like this is anything you are doing wrong, specifically considering that it is rather typical and natural for a mom to breastfeed their kid far longer than what many folks in the USA do.

- Consider your kid's pediatrician as the very best tool in assisting you in deciding to quit breastfeeding. They understand you, and they know your kid. They additionally understand your kid's health and well being. These are the tools required to make the proper decision about when to quit breastfeeding.

Every kid is distinct. Some kids wish to quit breastfeeding much sooner. When this holds true, let them do so. There is no reason to force it.

However, never ever permit somebody else to tell you when your kid ought to quit being breastfed. The reality is, your kid is going to assist you in making this choice naturally. It is most effective and most useful for the procedure to take place naturally to ensure that the kid and the mom are both well prepared for it.

Chapter 13: Transitioning From Breast Milk To A Cup

As you begin thinking about quitting to breastfeed your baby, you might be questioning how you are going to get them to avoid the bottle and go straight to the cup. There is truly no reason to need to place a breastfeed baby onto a bottle unless you are stopping them from all breastfeeding prior to the age of one. In this situation, it might be essential to think about the requirement for a bottle for a couple of months, or up until their physician advises that they no longer require a bottle whatsoever.

The initial step in making the shift from breastfeeding to the cup is to begin introducing the cup into their everyday lives. For instance, when the kid is in between 6 months and 9 months of age, the kid might have the ability to utilize a sip cup where they are ingesting a couple of ounces of breast milk, juice or water every day. Provide this to them throughout the day to assist satiate their thirst instead of feeding them. These cups must not meddle with their feedings. In case they do, the kid is getting too many of them.

For the next couple of months, keep utilizing the sippy cup. As you introduce increasingly more solid foods into the kid's diet plan, enable them to stop breastfeeding throughout the day. Enable them to consume breast milk, if you like, out of a sippy cup throughout the day with their solid food meals. This is going to depend, once again, on the age of the kid, however, many kids by the age of 9 months ought to be eating solid food. Work towards your pediatrician's objectives here, though. Keep breastfeeding during the night, such as right prior to bed. This makes it possible for that convenience and security to be offered to the kid.

As you go towards the end outcome, keep enabling the kid to wean from the breast naturally. You wish to permit this procedure to work up until it is most comfy for the kid to quit breastfeeding. For instance, your kid might wish to quit breastfeeding entirely due to the fact that he wishes to enjoy a film with his bro or sis instead of resting on mommy's lap.

When you enable this procedure to occur as naturally as possible, you are going to discover that it is satisfying to both you and them. Plus, it enables them to avoid needing to utilize a bottle entirely. This procedure is an outstanding advantage for every individual included.

Chapter 14: Medical Reasons For Baby Weaning

There are circumstances when it might end up being required for a person to quit breastfeeding for medical reasons. For instance, if you and your kid have actually been breastfeeding effectively for months, the odds are great that both of you have actually ended up being extremely connected to the procedure. Now, mommy has to take a medication that disrupts the breastfeeding procedure. What could be done? Before you just quit breastfeeding all at one time, it might be needed to work through the procedure thoroughly.

Can Something Else Be Done?

If you have actually been told by your physician that it is medically required to quit breastfeeding because of a medication you are taking, among the essential things to do is informing the physician about how that may not be a choice. For instance, if your kid has actually been nursing routinely and is not yet consuming a large quantity of food beyond breast milk, notify the physician. Numerous physicians are just not familiar with the baby weaning procedure and the significance of enabling the procedure to occur slowly. Learn if there is another medication that could be taken that is safe for baby. Oftentimes, this is a choice.

If you are not exactly sure if he medication you are taking is safe to take when you are breastfeeding, it is a much better choice to do some research initially. It is common for physicians who are not sure if you ought to be breastfeeding to merely state that you shouldn't be. Do some research by yourself, utilizing just dependable sources, obviously. It is typically an excellent idea to utilize the Doctor's Desk Reference for this kind of information. Additionally, you can call your pediatrician and ask them if you can breastfeed, taking the medications prescribed, because they are very likely to understand if you should or should not.

There might be circumstances when you merely need to quit breastfeeding right now. It could be brought on by the baby or due to something that happens. If there is a risk to the kid, do not do it, and work on weaning the baby. In case there is a possibility of weaning the kid gradually, take this path. It should be quite uncommon that the circumstance requires that you need to quit breastfeeding quickly. Most of the time, it is ideal to work gradually at the procedure to assist with shielding the kid from any prospective stress factors and to stay clear of any problems on your side, as well.

Chapter 15: Why Stopping Abruptly is a Bad Idea

Some parents decide one day that they just ought to be feeding their kid anything except breast milk. You might have spent the last couple of months of breastfeeding effectively. The issue is, you should never make the shift an abrupt one. This may do a great deal of harm to both you and your kid. Rather than pushing the scenario to take place immediately, it ought to be a steady procedure that is led not by the mom or dad yet rather by the kid themselves. This enables everyone involved to work through the procedure effectively.

The sudden baby weaning procedure does harm other moms. Initially, there is the psychological detachment that needs to be handled. Many others do not understand that their kid is really going to create so many problems when they are weaning. However, even the very best are going to go through a procedure of grieving for that loss of time together. However, along with this, there are other reasons why the mom is going to be jeopardized. For instance, if you quit nursing right now, your breasts are going to swell, and the end outcome is an agonizing engorging. This hurts when it occurs simultaneously. Additionally, it can get worse if you establish an infection or perhaps an abscess on your breast due to it.

While these conditions might look agonizing and unpleasant, a sudden baby weaning is going to do damage to the kid too. The initial and most substantial trauma is going to form the psychological trauma that the kid experiences. They have actually discovered this to be far more than simply their food source. They feel protected here. They are comforted by the mom's arms and their existence in general. If you take this away in a quick flash, the kid could be damaged mentally from it. You want to keep in mind that there is no way to inform your kid that it is all right since they do not totally comprehend vocal interactions at this moment.

Instead of deciding to quit nursing your kid immediately, keep in mind that the procedure could be done even more effectively if it is done slowly. This is going to enable the kid to enhance the desire to quit breastfeeding. The slow procedure additionally permits them to move some of their attachments to breastfeeding to other things and enables the mom's body to adapt much better to the procedure.

Chapter 16: The Procedure of Baby Weaning

How does baby weaning, in fact, take place? The procedure could be long and intricate, yet a brief version of the procedure could be explained in one word: gradual. Simply put, you and your kid ought to take the procedure gradually working towards the common objective of no longer breastfeeding yet enabling the kid to rely entirely on solid foods for their sustenance. The procedure additionally includes a lot of time to work through in regards to psychological stability. You and your kid have to both be prepared for the break, and you both ought to be physically able to make the shift.

Introducing The Process

As your kid grows older, his/her stomach gets bigger. They no longer have the ability to feel full from consuming simply breast milk. This might induce them to wish to breastfeed more frequently and gradually. You can end up being really overloaded by the procedure. This is when it ends up being time to introduce some solid foods to the kid's diet plan. The majority of babies are going to begin with an introduction to baby cereal, which is a product that breast milk might be added to so as to make it more appropriate to the kid. As soon as your physician states that you can present more solid foods into the kid's diet plan, have a go at it.

This is the initial step in the procedure of baby weaning. As quickly as the kid starts to consume some solid foods, you are going to have to be motivated to do so. Never ever permit the kid to attempt more than one kind of brand-new food in any 3-day duration as you want to be certaain that he/she is not allergic to the food. In time, integrate meals, where the kid is consuming 3 meals of baby food paired with fewer sessions at the breast for feeding. You are very likely to see that the baby is more happy to consume solid foods as they grow older.

Completing The Process

There is no easy procedure to quit breastfeeding completely. Rather, the procedure ought to be done as a gradual one, where the kid gradually begins to substitute their breast milk with solid foods. In doing so, the kid is going to end up being more familiar with consuming solid foods and is going to be less likely to be thinking about breastfeeding. Ultimately, you are going to have the ability to introduce cow's milk to the kid's diet plan as they are old enough. This could be an immediate substitute for breast milk for an older kid.

Chapter 17: Time for Night Weaning

For the majority of kids, the idea of quitting any feeding might appear crazy. In case you are a breastfeeding mommy, your kid is latched on good, and he/she is very likely acting as if they are starving with every feeding. How could you potentially believe the kid is prepared to be weaned from breastfeeding during the night? Regardless of why the kid is taking in these nutrients, it might be required for you to get more sleep. There are just so many nights that you can get no sleep before you burn out. Because of this, it might be required to begin promoting night weaning.

By the time your kid is approximately 4 to 6 months old, they ought to be capable of taking in ample calories throughout the day to break the night feeding. How do you know if your kid is prepared? Their age is a great sign. Some children are prepared prior to this, however, by this age, you can securely presume they are not going to go hungry. In case your kid is getting up during the night, remember that it might be since the kid's body has actually just ended up being used to waking up at that time. They might not be really getting up due to the fact that they are starving.

Are you prepared to quit night feedings? If you are succeeding with night feeding and you have the time to commit to it without it impacting your requirement for sleep and your general well being, there must not be a rush to quit feedings during the night. On the other hand, you wish to teach your kid to sleep properly throughout the night, and to do so, you are going to want to motivate them to sleep through it without, in fact, getting up for feedings.

Are you prepared to quit night feedings?

- Is the baby at least 4 months old?

- Is he/she taking in a great quantity of nutrients and calories throughout the day? Speak to your pediatrician to learn what is needed every day for your kid's age and size.

- Are you getting ample sleep? If not, you want to think about night weaning

In case you are still uncertain if you ought to quit night breastfeeding your kid, speak with your pediatrician about the procedure. You might be shocked to discover that your kid is prepared for the procedure, and you have the ability to get more sleep without robbing the kid.

Chapter 18: Tips For Natural Weaning

As a mom, your task is to offer the best to your kid. You have actually decided to enable your kid to quit breastfeeding naturally. The procedure is referred to as natural weaning, and you need to pay attention to the kid to see when he/she does not require breastfeeding any longer. This is maybe among the very best kinds of tools offered to ladies because it enables both the parent and the kid to be in a great situation when the decision to quit takes place.

To assist you with the procedure of natural breastfeeding, think about the following suggestions.

- Urge your kid to eat 3 full meals of solid food, plus treats throughout the day. As the kid grows older, you are going to wish to motivate them to rely upon these meals for their nourishment instead of breastfeeding. By the age of one year, kids ought to be consuming meals like this.

- Keep breastfeeding something separate from other meals. Breastfeed in only one place and do not urge the kid to link this location with food, yet only with breastfeeding. The less time you spend there, the less they are going to consider breastfeeding.

- Provide the kid with more time to be held and snuggling with you. You wish to motivate the kid to quit breastfeeding, however, if they are doing so due to the fact that they are hanging on to this time with you rather than utilizing it for food, they are most likely in requirement of more time with you throughout other parts of the day. Create time for you both to be close.

- You can still provide the baby weaning kid with breast milk in a cup if it enables you to assist them to feel great about the procedure. It can additionally assist you in breaking the requirement and dependence.

- Give the procedure time. It can take numerous months for a kid to, in fact, want to stop breastfeeding. Yet, it does not have to be something that is discussed so much as it is carried out naturally. When a kid has the ability to forget about the procedure, they feel great, and so do you about quitting.

Naturally, weaning your kid from the bottle is a crucial step in making it possible for that kid to establish completely. Yet, it is essential to enable the procedure to move effectively and slowly. By providing them with the say in when they have to breastfeed or not, the procedure is simpler.

Chapter 19: Night Weaning Your Baby

For those moms out there all set to quit breastfeeding their kid during the night, there is hope. Getting a good night's sleep suggests not needing to get up for a minimum of 6 hours per night. Anybody with a baby in the house is waiting on that day when the baby does not have to wake you up, and you can gently fall asleep in your bed. Yet, there comes a time when you might have to work to encourage this procedure to occur. There are lots of methods to get to the point of night weaning. Here are some pointers to assist you through the procedure.

1: Slow and Steady Wins The Race

It s essential to take the procedure of night weaning gradually. You wish to motivate the kid to quit the procedure slowly. An excellent procedure to start with is to merely begin offering the kid fewer minutes at each of the breasts. This enables them to get a tinier quantity of milk.

2: Increase the Length

If your baby gets up at 2 am every day to breastfeed, you might wish to begin pushing off the time when the kid is, in fact, breastfed. Lots of parents rush in to get the procedure began so they can return to sleep. Stay clear of this when night weaning. Rather, when the baby wakes you, attempt to comfort them with patting and calming them for 10 to 15 minutes prior to enabling them to breastfeed. They might fall back asleep without having to feed, too.

3: Provide The Kid With More Throughout The Day

Obviously, it is vital to guarantee your kid is getting ample nutrients throughout the day before beginning to wean from breastfeeding during the night. By doing this, the kid has the needed calories, and they are not starving when they get up. Kids additionally have to be motivated to quit and eat. As they age, they might stand up to eating at a scheduled time due to the fact that they wish to play. Motivate them to eat at that schedule, as it can motivate them to sleep better during the night when you do so.

Breastfeeding does not have to stop even if you are night weaning the baby. The advantage of night weaning is that it permits the kid to, in fact, stop waking up during the night to eat. You are going to discover that this is going to allow them to have excellent sleep patterns throughout the remainder of their lives, too.

Chapter 20: Weaning A Toddler If a Brand-new One Is On The Way

Moms typically need to balance 2 kids at the same time. If you are prepared to have another baby, or are pregnant, yet you have a toddler who is still nursing, this whole balancing ordeal can get slightly difficult. Besides, you want to be able to offer the baby the complete capability to nurse while still fulfilling the requirements of your toddler. While you may do both, you might discover that it is time for you to begin weaning the toddler from breastfeeding to ensure that you can begin working towards the objective of being prepared to provide for the brand-new baby.

To assist you through this procedure, here are a couple of actions. Amazingly, you might find yourself able to make this shift take place much easier than you anticipated, specifically if your toddler is at least 12 to 16 months old.

- Motivate more cup drinking. A toddler needs to know how to do this. Include cups during meals and make certain they have the ability to drink well from a cup prior to quitting breastfeeding.

- Motivate solid food eating in kids as they age, according to your pediatrician's suggestions. You want the kid to discover how to consume all solid foods.

- Make certain to satisfy the toddler's requirements for you. After all, they desire time with you more than they desire the breastfeeding nutrients. Hang out with the kid and snuggle with them. Having time together, such as this, without breastfeeding, is going to fulfill their psychological requirement for it.

- Get aid from daddy. He can assist the toddler in checking out brand-new foods, and if needed, he can begin bottle-feeding the kid.

- Talk with your physician about any issues you are having. The majority of kids are not going to have problems weaning from breastfeeding, however, some may. This might be an indication of the kid not getting ample nutrition throughout the day.

It might be feasible for you to nurse 2 babies at once, however, this procedure can tire you out and might leave the kids battling for you simultaneously. Rather than going down this path, you might wish to think about weaning the baby. This is possible, and it is going to help the toddler in getting used to somebody else getting the nursing from mommy by the time the baby arrives. Providing the kid with the convenience and security he/she requires is a really vital part of the procedure of weaning.

Chapter 21: What Happens When You Stop Breastfeeding?

Breastfeeding does not have to last for too long. Ultimately, your kid is going to stop breastfeeding, no matter if you are weaning them or if you are, in fact, enabling the procedure to occur naturally. Lots of ladies are dealing with the thought of what is going to occur to their breasts when they do quit breastfeeding. The idea of having soft breasts that merely droop is not something that is pleasing to anyone. There is no doubt that your breasts are going to be a little different, however, they do not always need to end up being unsightly.

There are lots of things that are going to determine what occurs to your breasts as you quit breastfeeding. Along with stopping to breastfeed, elements such as your age and your weight are going to impact this. Gravity, and even pregnancy itself, are going to impact the way your breasts look and feel. Each of these things is going to indicate what is going to occur as soon as you stop breastfeeding, too.

Throughout your pregnancy, your breasts need to get bigger so that they can accommodate the milk meant for the baby. Along with this bigger size, your nipples might additionally darken. Your areola might additionally darken. You might additionally discover that the nipples appear to be bigger. This is just one part of preparing for the baby. When you deliver, your breasts truly kick into gear. They are most likely going to feel much heavier to you, and you are going to observe that they appear to fill out more so. This is what occurs when your milk comes in. This generally occurs within a day or so of delivering.

Over the next couple of weeks, you might feel like your breasts are exceptionally big, however, this is going to pass. Typically, within the very first 2 to 3 weeks, the breasts are going to stay heavy like this. It is simply to guarantee that the baby has the ability to get as much as he/she requires, and it additionally enables your body to get used to the quantity of milk that is required. After these initial couple of weeks, your breasts are going to begin to get tinier and are going to remain this way up until you wean your kid.

What you might not wish to know is that your breasts are very likely to go back to their typical size, pre-pregnancy, as you wean from breastfeeding. Along with this change, you are going to discover they are not as young-looking or as lively as they once were. Nevertheless, there is no way to prevent this, unless you never ever get pregnant.

Chapter 22: Baby Weaning Explained

As a parent of a newborn, all you can actually think about is making certain that your baby is adapting well to breastfeeding. Before you know it, however, it is time to begin considering baby weaning. This is the procedure that all mammals have to go through. Every animal that nurses has to be capable of breaking away from the procedure ultimately to enable them to shift onto solid foods and eating on their own. While numerous moms and dads fear this procedure, it could be really constructive, and it is inescapable.

Why Is It Difficult?

The natural concern that somebody from the outside may have is this: Why is baby weaning such a complicated procedure? Why is it so difficult? The procedure is frequently complicated for a variety of reasons. Initially, lots of moms and dads see breastfeeding much differently than simply feeding their kid. The bond formed during this time is something special. Plus, this is a memorable time that moms and kids get to share collectively. Yet, even beyond this, there are other reasons that make it tough. Assisting a kid to change is not constantly a cut and dry procedure. Additionally, in some cases, the kid simply does not do well at the same time.

What To Do

There is much to discover about the procedure of baby weaning; however, the primary step is education. Before you begin to tackle this procedure by yourself, make it your objective to comprehend the numerous techniques available. Then, pick the ones you feel most comfy utilizing. Mom and kid are not the same, so it could be tough discovering that particular approach that works for you both. Yet, it is additionally essential to bear in mind that in a lot of circumstances, baby weaning does go off without a hitch. You can have a simple shift if you are prepared for it.

Take a while to think about the numerous baby weaning approaches. Most notably, invest time in the procedure yourself. Simply put, make sure you are mentally prepared for this shift, given that, usually, it is going to be the mom that has a hard time instead of the kid. Lastly, make sure you have aid. You are going to require assistance and support along the way. The bright side is that you can get this from your kid's dad, your household, and your friends. Additionally, there are exceptional resources available online to assist you, too.

Chapter 23: Why is Weaning Hard?

If you resemble many moms and dads, you actually would love a couple of additional months of keeping your kid as a baby. However, as they grow, you need to make decisions, consisting of decisions about weaning the kid. Weaning your kid could be a challenge, but for some individuals, the challenge is more difficult than for others. What might be behind this trouble? There might be numerous things; however, it is essential for you to understand what is occurring with your kid so that you can guarantee that the kid is mentally all right with the procedure.

For those moms who are having a problem with the weaning procedure, you might wish to take some additional time to find out why. Generally, a kid is going to resist to some degree, particularly if they are starving. In this case, you are going to want to guarantee the kid is being fed appropriately and is getting the essential calories he/she requires. Talk with your pediatrician about the amount of calories your kid requires for their age, size, and weight. As soon as you are sure they are getting the correct amount of calories, here are some other things to consider when struggling with breastfeeding weaning.

1. Is your kid having a hard time since he/she is not getting ample time with mommy? The kid might miss this intimate time and be craving it. 2. Have there been modifications in their schedule they are not getting used to? You ought to attempt to change one thing at a time for the kid to ensure that they do not feel like they remain in consistent flux. 3. Have you returned to work? Once again, if they are not getting their fill of mommy, they might begin attempting to breastfeed since this is a promise of cuddle and love time. 4. Is the kid ill? Some kids require convenience and "good feelings" that originates from being near to mommy when they are not feeling well. Kids that are sick are going to wish to nurse more than those that are well. 5. Observe any significant changes in your house? If so, this may be why your kid is having a hard time.

When there are no other indications that there is a problem, your kid might simply require more time. Provide the time they require. You might wish to stop attempting to breastfeed for a while, and after that, return to it in a month or so. They are going to stop breastfeeding ultimately; it simply depends upon when they are prepared to.

Chapter 24: When To Baby Wean

There are various viewpoints on when you ought to wean your kid from breastfeeding. The indications are all different and, in reality, you ought to consider this a procedure that is specific to you and to your kid. Each kid is really distinct in the way they feel and respond to baby weaning. By many accounts, the very best way to understand if your kid is prepared to wean is to permit the procedure to occur naturally. This is, in fact, how most moms and kids are going to go through the procedure, and it is most likely to be the very best path for you and your kid to go through, as well.

It is optimal for your baby to just grow out of breastfeeding. This is natural weaning, often referred to as a baby-led weaning. It is necessary to understand what your baby requires, as each kid is distinct. You might discover that your kid requires more time than your initial kid to make this break from breastfeeding. If you take a look at your kid's other locations of advancement, you might currently understand what the kid is going to require. For instance, some kids demand to be held more. Other kids like to play alone. You would not typically force a kid to establish in a different way in these other areas, which implies you actually should not do so at this moment either. It is important that you permit the kids to grow as they naturally would.

Do not set a time for how long your kid is going to nurse. Attempt to be more versatile about the whole procedure. This procedure ought to be one that takes place as naturally as feasible so that there is no restriction or risk for either of you throughout the procedure. Do you understand what the initial step in the procedure is? The initial step is as straightforward as providing your kid with his/her very first bites of food.

As you begin thinking of baby weaning, understand that this is not the first occasion. Unlike giving that very first bite of food, the procedure is not something that you simply choose to do one day. Rather, it is a procedure that typically takes a couple of months of adjusting and a slow-moving one at that. Offer your kid the capability to grow and establish as it feels appropriate to do. This eventually is going to offer you and him the very best capability to overcome baby weaning together.

Baby weaning is a delightful procedure when done so.

Chapter 25: When To Night Wean

Night weaning is a procedure that includes helping a breastfed baby to stop taking feedings during the night. Similar to babies who are bottle-fed, the procedure is a good one for the kid. You want the kid to sleep through the night without having to get up to take a feeding. Each kid is distinct in regards to the length of time it is going to take for them to sleep through the whole night. However, it is frequently essential to take actions that move procedure along. Bear in mind that night weaning just impacts the night. The majority of moms and dads are going to wish to think about feeding their baby throughout the day by breast.

A kid is most likely to sleep through the night provided that they have ample calories in their system to keep them pleased throughout the night. This is not something that the majority of kids are going to have the ability to do within the very first weeks of their lives merely since they are too young and have stomachs that are too little. Generally, by the time a kid is 4 to 6 months of age, they are taking in ample calories throughout the day, and they should not require feeding during the night for at least 5 to 6 hours at a time. Some babies might have to feed for longer, and some babies are going to night wean far earlier than this.

Some babies require feeding during the night by breast due to the fact that they require this not just for the food, but for the nearness it permits them. For instance, maybe you have actually returned to work. Your kid is now seeing you less and bonding with you less. They might get up during the night wishing to breastfeed, not since they are starving, yet most likely since the kid wants to hang on to more time with mommy. This could be a typical requirement particularly as your kid establishes mentally.

Put in the time to approach night feeding. Do not attempt to push the scenario on your kid because he/she is not very likely to take to this well. Rather, they will keep waking you up until they are pleased that they are getting ample attention from you. Night weaning can and ought to be taken into consideration when your kid is old enough and wants to wean. You can begin the procedure as soon as the kid reaches between 4 and 6 months of age.

Baby Sleep

Essentials

Parent's Guide to Methods and Tips for Establishing a
Safe Sleeping Environment and Habits for a Good Night's
Sleep to Ensure Your Baby Grows Up Healthy, Happy and
Self-Assured

By Laura Nicol

Introduction to Baby Sleep Essentials

Chapter 1: What You Have To Understand About Baby Sleeping

Your baby will be sleeping a lot. Throughout the initial couple of months, your baby is going to sleep for the majority of the day. You might not get any actual interaction or responses aside from crying and sleep.

Sleep

After a couple of months, your baby has to be placed on a basic regimen. Typically, this consists of wind down time, feeding, bath, massage, and sleep. You can constantly utilize relaxing music to assist your baby to sleep and even stuffed animals that make the noises of the wombs in their belly. Make sure not to put the stuffed animals into her crib, as that is unsafe.

SIDS and Sleeping Bags

SIDS, Sudden Infant Death Syndrome is a syndrome wherein an otherwise relatively healthy baby, all of a sudden, passes away in sleep. There are things you may do to stop SIDS. Remember to always put your baby on his rear to sleep. Put the baby in well-fitted clothes and do not place any pillows, blankets, or toys into the baby's crib.

Attempt New Things

Attempt various things and see which works finest for you. Try the baby sleeping in your bed, co-sleeper, bassinet, and crib and see which one the baby naturally adjusts to. Then weekly, you can attempt a brand-new sleeping source and observe if the baby is going to sleep in that.

Your Marriage

Even if you have a brand-new baby, that does not imply you should not be placing effort into your marriage. It is still crucial to spend time with your partner, both with the baby and independently.

Talk, laugh, have a good time, make love, simply delight in one another.

Guidance

Take in the guidance of your physicians and your parents. You can read books on how to get your baby to sleep. Eventually, however, you are going to understand what works ideally for your brand-new youngster. So unwind and have a good time. What might sometimes appear like a great deal of work to get your baby to stop crying and begin sleeping, you are going to just experience for a while with your kid. Simply adore them and delight in these brand-new experiences.

Chapter 2: Everything About Baby Sleeping Bags

Have you heard of the baby sleeping bags or baby sacks? They are a prominent item in Europe, and now it's made its way to the USA!

SIDS

Baby sleeping bags, if developed and fitted correctly, are thought to aid in protecting against SIDS. This is because of the reality that baby is still kept warm, without the concern of a blanket coming too near to their face, and protecting against airflow. Doctors emphasize that a proper sleep sack has a fitted neck, guaranteeing that the baby can not slip within. Sleep sack also needs to be sleeveless to enable correct airflow, and it does not have a hood. You merely dress your baby in regular sleepwear and zip them into this wearable blanket.

Firms

Various firms provide various designs from standard to luxurious, vibrant, light-weight, included warmth. You can even buy natural baby sleeping bags if you choose to dress your baby in an environment-friendly outfit. The natural baby sacks do not skimp on the design either. They have really adorable patterns also. The majority of the reliable baby sleeping bag firms show their guidelines on their website in case they satisfy the physician's requirements. The materials could be something as standard as one hundred percent to cotton, to flannel, fleece and even silk.

Customers

Users of these baby sleeping bags speak highly of them. They think they are the one item you require for your baby to sleep through the night. The baby sleeping bags additionally have the included function of keeping the baby from climbing outside of the crib. The zippers are created so that curious kids can not undo them. Despite the fact that their legs are covered, they can move them inside the sack. Nevertheless, they are not created to be strolled in and can, for that reason, supply you with an assurance that when your baby gets up, they can not climb outside of the crib.

These items actually are a fantastic idea, and for some, a unique approach really isn't needed. Simply put the baby in the baby sleeping bags, and the baby is going to start sleeping through the night. What if it truly is as straightforward as this? What if this Baby Sleeping Bag can lastly supply you and your baby with a comfy night's sleep.

Chapter 3: Baby Sleeping and Intimacy

It is necessary to make sure that your baby's sleep practices are not impacting your marriage's intimacy. Your baby is now the middle of your world, however, your marriage can still share that limelight.

Speak With Your Partner

Make certain that in order to relieve any sensations of jealousy in between your partner and your baby, and there may be some, you still offer your partner attention. Speak with him about things aside from your baby. Speak about sports, or golf, or something you understand he is going to delight in.

Stop Talking

Among the very best things to do if your baby's sleep is impacting the intimacy your partner and you used to have, is to simply stop talking and touch. Let him understand that you desire him. It is necessary to still make love. If the baby is getting up in the middle of the night, attempt making love in the early morning, while the baby is still asleep. Also try it when your partner gets home from work, and the baby is resting.

Start

Go on dates with one another still. Being a parent is a terrific thing, however, being an excellent other half and partner to each other is an outright requirement. You can go to dinner and get dressed up as you used to for a date. You can even have a relied-upon sitter keep an eye on your child or one of your parents while you have a great night or weekend away from town with one another. Even if you take the baby out of town with you, it is necessary to still go on a date, even though the baby is now with you. A fantastic little trip, even for a night, can make a substantial distinction in how your baby's sleep pattern is impacting intimacy.

Touch

It is necessary that after the baby is born, you keep on touching your partner in a relaxing manner. A kiss occasionally, or resting on the sofa beside one another while holding hands are fantastic means to show each other that although baby may be keeping you up in the evening, you still desire one another.

Love

Keep on telling one another how you appreciate each other and demonstrate it. Do not simply utilize words. Surprise your partner with tickets to the big game.

Chapter 4: Getting Your Baby To Sleep

Do you wish to make it a lot easier for your kids to go to sleep? It actually could be easy, simply be arranged and constant. The following actions are going to assist you.

Wear Them

Wear your baby in a baby sling on your body for approximately thirty minutes prior to bedtime. This is going to make your baby feel comfy. There are several choices when it pertains to baby slings. You just need to pick what you are comfy with. Keep the baby in front of you and additionally ensure that the baby's face is uncovered to assist them in breathing properly.

Bath

Provide the baby with a relaxing bath prior to bedtime. Utilize soothing or essential oils to assist with unwinding the baby even further. Even though he does not appear to like the bath the very first time, do not quit. The very first bath may be extremely frightening for the baby and for you. Babies are small, and their skin is soft, it gets incredibly slippery when damp.

Massage

Administer a couple of drops of natural essential oil to the cream base you utilize and see your baby's responses as you provide a massage. Rub your hands carefully all over the child. See what he likes and what he does not and adapt. Beware when rubbing over his little stomach if he just ate. You might discover he has gas, or that the tummy is full. A back rub is a terrific means for a baby to unwind. Ensure that you turn their head to the side to ensure that their breathing is never ever restricted. You can quickly provide a massage while the baby is resting, however, more than likely, the newborn is going to wish to feel your heat, so you can administer the cream while he is laying down, and after that, you can hold him in your arms and massage.

Voice Soothing

Speak to the small baby, allowed him to look up at you with those small eyes, and look straight back into his eyes. Your face could be a terrific learning instrument for the baby, and he is going to end up being captivated. You wish for the baby to count on you, so talk or sing him lullabies.

Sacks

Attempt placing your baby into a baby specialized baby sack or a sleeping bag. It might be what you have actually been yearning for to get your baby to sleep.

Chapter 5: More Tips To Get Your Baby To Sleep

Does it seem like you are attempting every little thing to get your baby to sleep throughout the night? If you have not currently attempted these pointers, they are terrific.

Feed Your Baby Throughout The Day

You wish to train your baby to comprehend that daytime is for eating, and nighttime is for sleeping. Lots of babies delight in awakening to merely feel their mom's comfort and delight in some breast milk. It ends up being a convenience and need for babies who understand that they are going to now get it during the night. Numerous babies get so occupied throughout the day playing and finding brand-new things, and they forget to eat. This is where you come in. Feed your baby every 3 hours. To break the routine of waking to eat during the night, you ought to offer a complete feeding at the initial waking.

Offer The Baby A Calm Day

Are you extremely stressed out? Are you constantly in a rush? You may be leaving the baby at daycare way too much. Daycare may not be the best match for your baby. Attempt and provide the baby with a calm day. Opt for long strolls to relax your baby.

Father Down

Put your baby's head versus the front of your neck with your chin leaning on the baby's head. The vibrations of the voice can set the baby to sleep. In case this does not work, rest with the baby in an identical position and let the baby drop off to sleep on your chest. When the baby is entirely asleep, place the kid onto the bed. You can snuggle with the baby, and after that, carefully move away.

Wear The Baby, Literally

Research studies have actually revealed that babies who are worn in a baby sling drop off to sleep much better than babies who are not. About half an hour prior to baby's bedtime, wear the baby around your home. Ensure she is totally sleeping, and after that, put her into her baby crib.

Swaddle

Babies like their clothing to be tight. You are going to more than most likely get a lesson on how to swaddle by the nurses prior to leaving the healthcare facility. Older babies like for their clothing to be looser. Adapt the layer of clothes properly and dress a little one in one hundred percent cotton.

Chapter 6: Baby Sleeping and Family

Everybody will have a viewpoint on how to get your baby to go to sleep. You may wish to have a go at the guidance of your parents and see how that goes.

Parental Guidance

Your parents raised you. You may have an identical sleep pattern as your baby. You can ask your parents if they have any suggestions or tips that they can offer you on assisting your baby fall and remain asleep.

Try It

Attempt to see if their guidance works. Your mother may be able to offer you a comprehensive strategy of precisely what the regimen was that used to work for you. Give it a try bit by bit. See if you get any outcomes.

Modification

If you observe that your baby now sleeps an additional hour longer, that is fantastic! After you attempt your mother's set regimen, make a couple of modifications. If you are used to providing the baby with feedings during the night, go with a complete feeding after the initial waking up duration, and see if that relieves the baby. After feeding, make certain that you alter the baby's diaper. It could be that something as minor as a damp diaper making your baby so aggravated that she can't handle it and has crying bouts during the night because of that.

Little Measures

In case you usually have the baby sleeping in bed with you, attempt utilizing a bassinet or a co-sleeper. These are great options to free up your own individual bed space, however, still make it possible for the baby to be near. Co-sleepers connect at mattress level aside from your bed. Co-sleepers could be useful as you have the capability to connect and relieve your baby, and after that, fall right back to sleep. A bassinet resembles a little baby crib, typically with a canopy on top. You can put the bassinet in your room, and she is going to just be a couple of steps away. You and your partner are going to have the whole bed to yourselves; however, you are going to feel safe now the baby is still in your bedroom.

Unwind

Simply unwind; in case you are consistent, your baby is going to find out how to go to sleep. Ensure you are consistent and adhere to a regimen.

Chapter 7: Allergies and Baby Sleeping

Is the reason your baby is not sleeping due to the fact that she is allergic to something that is keeping her up? Allergies can impact a baby in a huge and unpleasant way, and result in unpleasantness through the night.

What Is An Allergy?

An allergy is an immune response to the compound, referred to as an allergen. Allergy can vary from moderate, consisting of pollen to a serious and deadly anaphylactic shock. Typical allergies vary from hay fever to bugs, drugs to food. Lots of allergies can trigger asthma and induce lethal anaphylactic shock caused by food allergies that can induce death. When an irritant impacts your baby by touching, eating, breathing, or injection, the body sees it as a damaging intruder and launches histamines and chemicals to combat it.

What Are the Signs?

- Watery eyes

- Blockage

- Runny nose

- Coughing, especially during the night

- Swelling of the skin

- Red, inflamed skin

- Sneezing

Skin and blood tests carried out by your medical professional can additionally diagnose an allergic reaction.

What May be Inducing an Allergic Reaction?

Practically anything can induce an allergic reaction in the delicate and still establishing baby immune system. Typical reactors are dust, mold, milk, animal dander, nuts, eggs, detergent, baby wash, clothing material. Mommy's breast milk is a much better option, as some baby formulas can induce a response.

What To Do About An Allergic Reaction

Never ever, ever ignore the intensity of an allergic reaction. Allergies can vary from irritating annoyance to a dangerous issue; it might additionally be what is keeping your infant from sleeping through the night. Allergies and asthma might be inducing your kid's physical pain, or the failure to breathe. Asthma is a persistent condition of the breathing system. The air passage swells, and breathing ends up being tough.

Asthma can take place day-to-day or in unforeseen outbursts. Food allergy insomnia is a sleep condition brought on by an intolerance to a kind of food. Allergic reactions impact over 20% of the U.S. population. If either parent has allergic reactions or asthma, the infant might have acquired these conditions. As usual, the very best thing to carry out is to consult your baby's doctor. If the response happens right away after contact, for instance, if your child's hands start to swell or she starts coughing right after consuming a particular kind of food, that might be your allergen. The very best thing to do is to stay clear of contact entirely. If the infant's signs happen after communicating with a pet, the animal might need to be put outside or in the garage.

Chapter 8: Enough is Enough

When is enough, enough? When is it time to begin to attempt the methods of baby sleeping alone? That depends upon your baby and you. It is enough, when the delights of having a baby sleeping near to you, or waking you up during the night, really begin to impact your partner and you.

Nobody Else

It actually has nothing to do with other individuals. In case you are attempting to contend with other households, it's a wild-goose chase. This has to be about your own family's requirements. You have to be able to kick back and ask if this is the correct time to have more stress in your life. Or is it the ideal time to remove some stress by having a baby sleep in their room, in their baby crib.

Communicate

The only solution to a delighted family, a delighted marriage, and a delighted baby is through communication. Speak with your partner and let them understand that you're uncertain if it's a good time today to have the brand-new child sleeping alone. Be truthful. Request their viewpoint. In case they are determined, allow them to explain why.

Weigh Your Choices

Assess the choices that you do have. You can keep on living with a baby in between you in both terrific and not so terrific ways, or right down the hall. Perhaps you feel its' time to have the baby sleeping on his own due to the fact that it's taking a toll on your intimacy. Perhaps you liked the sensation of being in just one another's arms on special nights, without a baby weeping.

Do Not Let It Impact Love Making

Despite the fact that you have a baby, that does not indicate you have to stop making love. You can definitely make love in other parts of your house besides your bed. And you can make love with each other while the baby is sleeping.

Decide

You ought to arrive at a conclusion together. In case you both believe that things are alright, and other aspects of your intimate relationship aren't being impacted by the baby's sleeping, then maintain things as they are for some time. In case it isn't working, swing into action and get the things going to get baby sleeping in his own part of the home.

Chapter 9: Refusing to Sleep

This may be the largest issue when it concerns baby sleep: refusing to sleep. There are even several grownups who definitely despise the concept of sleeping. They are going to push it off, frequently dropping off to sleep on the sofa, and even while taking a seat having a discussion!

When a kid refuses to head to sleep, they deny themselves of sleep required to grow and you and your partner of necessary rest and alone time. This might just be a persistent kid who does not wish to rest. It is essential to have a reasonable bedtime, around 8 pm. You merely need to adhere to a regimen, allow them to learn about a routine, and soothe them, so they actually want to hit the hay.

There are indications of a drowsy kid. A yawn is definitely one of them. Red or saggy eyes are others, along with tears prior to bedtime. It is as if their bodies closed down, and the only things that appear to function are their tear ducts and voice. Thumb sucking and tumbling onto the flooring are additional signs that your kid is tired.

You let them understand it is 5 minutes up until a bath. The bath could be one that consists of lavender for unwinding the baby. After that, tell them when there are 2 minutes left before leaving the bath. Once they remain in bed, tell them you are going to read them a story, and after that, they are going to hit the hay. Do not be amazed if they are unexpectedly thirsty. Offer them a glass of water prior to their bath and nighttime potty trip. Then put them in their bed, kiss them good night, let them know you love them, and leave. If they leave the bed, do not snap, just walk them back into the area and into their bed and leave. This might take a bit of discipline, however, you are going to ultimately wear them out. Kids are going to attempt every technique in the book, from I want milk, to my clothes are scratchy. They are going to attempt to wear you down with their cuteness. However, remind yourself that they require sleep, and so do you. They require it to grow as they should. You and your partner have to destress and reenergize.

Chapter 10: Teething and Baby Sleeping

Can you picture just how much of a trouble it would be to have a dreadful tooth pain while attempting to sleep? Attempt and picture it for your baby.

Teething is the procedure through which the baby's teeth start breaking through the gums. This procedure might be what is impacting your baby's capability to sleep. The basic teething duration can be between 3 months and 12 months. Even prior to the three-month mark, the baby might start to demonstrate indications of early teething.

The Teething Indications

- Loss of appetite

- State of mind is poor

- Gums are inflamed or bruising

- Chews on things

- Extreme salivating

The very best method to inspect if a baby is teething is to perform the gum-massage test. Your baby is going to, more than likely, permit a finger around their gum lines. You put your finger along the baby's gum line and feel for inflamed ridges of pre-teething gums. Babies' responses to teething differ, some are once a month teethers to, and some do it sporadically. The most agonizing instance might additionally be the most apparent: when numerous teeth start to come in simultaneously.

Sleeping While Teething

Throughout the day, have a go at a teething ring, a water-filled rubber teething toy. Make certain it is a real teether and not a tinier toy that might induce your kid to choke. Mommy or daddy's fingers can additionally assist by administering mild pressure along the gum line. A cold spoon, while held by mommy or daddy, might assist with the teething procedure. Cold food consisting of cooled applesauce, cool frozen fruit juice, yogurt pureed peaches, and a popsicle can assist in relieving the baby's tooth discomfort. If the baby awakens throughout the middle of the night, the very best thing to carry out is to use a cool teething ring or fingers and alleviate and hold the baby up until the baby is totally asleep.

Consult Your Physician

An excellent pediatrician is a blessing. The very best method to assist your infant in sleeping when teething is via medication. Prior to putting your kid on medication, you ought to talk to your physician for the correct guidelines.

Chapter 11: Fantastic Routines for Baby Sleeping

Do you wish to know about some things you can use throughout the day to ensure your child sleeps through the night? Here are 5 habits that you can attempt down the road.

1. Encourage a Busy Day

Throughout the day, engage your infant via household lights and sounds. Depending upon their age, you can have a play date, take them to a park or to the beach.

2. Keep an Eye on the Naps

Naps are terrific for children. It provides a chance to rest, and you with a chance to sleep or get things done around your home. Ensure the kid is not sleeping for too long; however, as long patches of sleep might seriously interrupt their nighttime regimen.

3. Nighttime Regimen

Have a nighttime regimen. Always wash your child. Some children enjoy the warm water, others are horrified. Attempt a lavender bath to unwind infant and assist him in sleeping. After bathing, snuggle with the infant, glide in your chair, and read or sing to the child. Be regular with music you play for the infant at bedtime as well.

4. Infant's Natural Sleep Clock

Some infants are night owls, while others are early birds. In case you observe a natural pattern forming with the infant, adapt your regimen to fit the child.

5. Pacifiers

Pacifiers are excellent choices, and might even protect against the risk of SIDS, sudden infant death syndrome. Pacifiers aid in keeping the child sucking during the night, however, the parent may additionally be continuously awakening to put the pacifier back into the child's mouth when it falls out. If you pick a pacifier, you may be able to merely place the infant back to sleep by putting the pacifier back in the mouth, rather than picking her up and letting her understand that she just needs to cry to be held.

There are lots of choices you have when it pertains to attempting to get your child to sleep. They are all truly based upon your inclinations and what you are comfy with, for your partner, you and your infant. You might wish to attempt various options to see what you like the best, or what you believe is most helpful. However, it is necessary regardless of what you select to be consistent for the best outcomes.

Chapter 12: Child Sleeping Organically

Do you wish for your infant to go to sleep while just utilizing environmentally friendly items? Now you have lots of choices to discover the very best natural items for you.

Research

Do your research. Ensure that your natural items truly are created from natural cotton and are soft, to ensure that they do not irritate your child's extremely tender skin.

Have a Good Time

There are numerous natural sites now that offer you a one-stop shopping spot for all of your natural baby requirements. Have a good time taking a look at the numerous websites. Organic is not what it is used to be! There are now lots of trendy and safe items offered to you and your child. You are going to be surprised by the intense colors and soft materials of bed linen, clothes, and even toys.

Feed Her

You can even now acquire organic food and formula. The very best food for your child is your own natural breast milk. There is a big selection of food to pick from for a baby that's a bit older, featuring natural yams, cereal, applesauce, and peaches. You can discover natural baby food from firms, such as Gerber's.

Bathe Her

You can even utilize natural items on your baby's skin. Aveeno has a terrific baby care line that is created with natural components and oatmeal. They even provide fantastic moisturizers for mommy. Utilizing these items is not going to make you afraid that the items you are placing on your own hands and body are going to aggravate your child's tender skin.

Make certain that you utilize one hundred percent natural cotton material in clothes, car seat covers, and shopping carts. Organic cotton is going to be without artificial chemicals and pesticides. Try to find special natural items to aid your child's sleep, consisting of natural baby sleeping bags. Ensure that these zipped up garments have the appropriate security precautions, consisting of a zipper the young child can't unzip. You might feel fantastic understanding that your child is being exposed to plenty of natural products. You might discover that your child sleeps much easier since any irritants that might have been present previously are now gone. Make certain to constantly let your kid understand you love her, and you just desire what's finest for her with natural products. It is going to be a wild trip, and now you can make it a natural one that results in much better sleep for the baby.

Chapter 13: Baby Sleeping Methods

There are several methods you can utilize when attempting to get your child to sleep much better, or through the night.

Cry-It-Out

There is the old-fashioned cry-it-out method that lots of people do not like. You merely allow your infant to cry all night long up until it goes to sleep on its own. This strategy is discredited due to the fact that there is an absence of connection and caring that might impact your kid's capability to trust you.

Controlled Crying

The controlled crying method is utilized by comprehending what kind of cry deserves attention. If the child is crying in distress, constantly go to her and discover what is inducing the discomfort. This cry is going to be a constant high pitched cry or low groan. Nevertheless, it is going to be constant. The other kind of cry is more than likely what your child is doing now. It is called the attention cry. It might begin and then stop briefly, as though the child is awaiting a response, followed by another cry. You are expected to calmly enter into the area, keep the lights off, stroll to the baby crib, stay clear of eye contact, and carefully run your hand along the child's back, whisper "shh" and step back out. You are going to discover that the infant is going to stop crying, and after that, begin crying once again, either in a couple of minutes or an hour. Make sure to space out your time to ensure that each time is further apart than the previous time.

No Crying

Some parents merely can't stand the noise of their infant sobbing. They simply wish to stop what seems like discomfort. If the child is giving an attention cry, there is no discomfort, he simply desires convenience. Some parents pick the infant up and hold it up until it returns to sleep.

Whatever approach you pick depends on you. You can normally see the very best outcomes with the controlled crying method. The cry-it-out method can just feel neglectful. Merely try and remain calm when it pertains to your infant sleeping and your child crying. You might feel aggravated due to the fact that you are additionally tired. Attempt and depict to your kid that you love him, and that you wish to relieve him. It might be the very best method that you can utilize, one that is full of love.

Chapter 14: The 5 S's To Baby Sleeping

The Happiest Child on the Block Technique established by Harvey Karp, MD. Dr. Karp thinks that infants were born during a time when they are, in fact, in a "4th trimester" and are not totally established. He created a series of methods, which, when done with specific accuracy, can get a child to drop off to sleep and sleep for 1-2 hours longer.

Dr. Karp's belief is that these techniques recreate the firmness of the womb.

1. Swaddling

Firm swaddling recreates the firm touch and heat that the infant now misses from the womb.

2. Side/Stomach Position

Put your child, while still holding her, perhaps on her left side to assist with food digestion, or on her stomach to support the baby. When she is asleep, you can securely put her into her baby crib on her rear to protect against SIDS.

3. Shushing Sounds

These white noise sounds are similar to the noises heard inside the womb, that is a whooshing noise triggered by the blood streaming through the arteries near the womb. A hairdryer, vacuum cleaner, and fan can reenact the noise, or you can buy the white noise CD.

4. Swinging

The infant was used to the moving stimulation of the womb, and to be taken out from it is a shock to the infant's system. Care rides and rocking can substitute this. This movement is very relaxing, and your infant has a difficult time adapting to it not being there.

5. Sucking

The sucking that an infant does has impacts on the nerve system. It activates a soothing reflex and launches natural chemicals to the brain. Sucking could be done with a pacifier, bottle, breast, or finger.

This method could be incredibly helpful. If you require more, you can browse Dr. Harvey Karp's name and discover videos of him doing the method. He emphasizes that there is a particular accuracy required in order for the method to be reliable. He commits his life to studying children, and the method does work. It is vital to watch him doing it to ensure that you recreate it in properly and do not induce your child any damage.

Chapter 15: The Controlled Crying Method

Potentially the most effective method to get a kid to drop off to sleep is through the Controlled Crying Method. This is not the identical thing as leaving a kid to sob. With this method, you have the ability to acknowledge if the kid desires convenience or attention or if they may require a diaper change.

Controlled crying could be difficult for moms and dads to do due to the fact that many parents do not wish to listen to their child cry. This leads to an emotional panic, where the mom and dad feel the requirement to relieve, and shield. You might believe that you are losing control, and sense a surge of adrenaline. It is just your body's response to hearing your infant crying.

Comprehending The Cry

There are 2 kinds of cries. If your kid is crying in a constant high-pitched cry or a low, groaning one, then the kid ought to be tended to. The kid might be in extreme distress or discomfort. If your kid cries such as this, look at her right away to see what the matter is. Crying for attention, or for convenience sounds different than the pain cry. It starts as a whimper or wail, and then splits into intervals as if the kid is waiting on the outcome or response. Picture it as a pattern of crying, waiting, and crying once again. Up until you can acknowledge the distinction in between the cries, it is not advised to attempt this method.

Method

The very first time you hear the kid cry, spend a couple of minutes listening, it is going to be tough not to pick him up. In case the crying is not distressed, head to the kid after a good quantity of time. Do not switch on the light, talk or make eye contact, take a look at the belly or nose. This might be really difficult to do. Merely whisper "shh," and rub his back or belly. Change the covers and leave. Your kid is going to wake up and cry once again, wait for twice as long to go to him and do the identical thing. When it occurs once again, wait for twice as long, and after that, do it again. This is going to most likely remain a very challenging method to master since you just wish for your infant to go to sleep. It might not get much easier for you, however it could be incredibly effective. The outcomes ought to be observed in about one week.

Chapter 16: Home Remedies For Baby Sleeping

Have you ever asked yourself if there any home remedies you may do that are going to assist your infant in sleeping throughout the night? There are a couple.

Baby Bath

The bath could be an exceptionally calming location for a child. Utilize a mild product like Aveeno to clean their tender skin. While you are drying the child, you can put a couple of drops of lavender within the bathwater and run it once again, on warm. The lavender odor is going to fill the washroom and might unwind your child as you towel dry her. While the tub is filling again, take in the aromatherapy steam and carefully rock your child and sing.

Baby Massage

You can drop a couple of drops of that identical lavender or mandarin oil into your child's delicate baby cream. These 2 oils are relaxing and have a sedative result, rendering it simpler for the kid to sleep. You can offer your child a massage. Do it much lighter than you would usually because babies are small and tender. Massage the baby oil over. She is going to enjoy the feel of this, and it might assist her to sleep through the entire night.

Swaddle

After your infant is all smooth and soft, swaddle her firmly to ensure that she can feel that soothing heat she was so used to in the womb. Sing calming lullabies, or simply talk with her in a soft voice. Let her understand you adore her with all your soul. She is going to feel your love. Despite the fact that a sobbing infant can often be discouraging, envision how tough it is for her to adapt to this huge brand-new world. Merely take pleasure in the truth that you get to snuggle with a gorgeous child in order to enhance the child's sleep.

When attempting essential oils and brand-new baby items, you may wish for her to sleep with you to guarantee nothing bad takes place. You have to be sure that any essential oil is precisely what it claims to be. Make certain it is natural. You do not wish to aggravate the infant's skin. Relaxing oils like mandarin and lavender ought to be great since they are mild, however, one can never ever be too cautious.

Chapter 17: How To Place Your Kid To Bed Quickly

So, your kid will not sleep, or you simply desire a simpler method to place them to bed? In either case, there are some basic actions in order to get your kid into bed. Stick to this regimen, and ultimately, your kid is going to have the ability to do it on its own.

Unwind

All occasions leading up to bedtime have to be in a wind-down setting. Voices ought to be quieter, playing ought to be less unruly, and the general tone ought to be calm. Just as an adult discovers it challenging to go right to sleep if she is riled up, it is the same for a kid.

Bath Time

Draw a bath and allow the kid to understand it is time to take a bath. Additionally, offer him a hint when it is nearly time to get out. When it is time to get out, involve the kid in the regimen. Ask him to pull the plug for you, even his ducky can assist, and emphasize that he is doing an excellent job.

Bedtime Story

This is a good time to pull out a fantastic bedtime story. Let her pick a book, however, just offer her a couple of options. If she has a favorite, then read it, repeatedly. If you tell fantastic fairy tales without using a book, do so. You can captivate her in either kind of story.

Communicate

In some cases, the kid wishes to talk after a story. This is essential, have him lay back and unwind. He can tell you about his day, and you can offer him recognition. Tell him he has actually been excellent at listening recently. You can even discuss your day tomorrow.

Correspond

In case you and your partner are rotating, ensure you both follow the regimen. Do not go to sleep with your kid, merely let the kid know it's lights out soon. She ought to be sleepy and unwinded. The lively kid may push for more. The very best thing to do is assure her that you are going to be there in the early morning and that she is excellent and you adore her.

Chapter 18: Is Baby's Sleeping Impacting Other Kids?

Ask yourself this, do your other kids appear a bit resentful of the infant's sleeping patterns? Maybe the brand-new kid is keeping the older teens awake on school nights. Perhaps 7-year-olds do not like that the child receives the care that she used to receive. See if there happens to be an alteration in mindset right prior to bedtime.

Recognize The Issue

Notice if there is a huge alteration in habits with your teens or other kids about 20 minutes before the newborn goes to sleep. You may observe a minor annoyance or perhaps an extreme alteration in habits. Do not make a teen get up during the night to check on the sleeping infant. That is not their task. That is your task.

Attempt A Various Regimen

Attempt to change it up a bit. In case you usually have the child sleeping in your bed, attempt placing her in a bassinet rather. In case you usually let her cry, do not. Whatever it is you are doing, simply see if the other kids' conduct changes if you alter it for approximately a week.

Envy

Among the significant issues with having a newborn is that other kids can end up being exceptionally envious. Do not think it is just a youngster that this behavior can stem from. Older kids can feel that they are being ignored, too, and that all of the focus is now on the brand-new child. Even your partner can feel envious. If before the child was born, you offered your partner a great deal of attention, make certain that does not change. It may be something that you need to work out, however, it can quickly be repaired. It is additionally essential to take care of any envious behavior. Let the other kids understand that it is not fine to be envious, that there is ample love to go around for everybody. You can integrate the brand-new infant into activities, however, make sure to ensure there is still alone time with other kids. Keep in mind at all times that you are the parent, and you decide. It depends on you to adapt to the sleeping pattern of a kid. And you might need to make changes so as to see any improvements; it is simply the essence of being a parent.

Chapter 19: Several Bedtimes

What do you do if you are attempting to put a child to sleep in addition to a 3-year-old and a 5-year-old? You use extremely regular regimens, at 3 separate times. It can get challenging, however, each kid requires different attention, and it is going to work.

Little One

Wash your smallest one initially. You can breastfeed or offer him a bottle. Make certain he is all tight and warm and rock on your rocking chair, or utilize the glider. While this is occurring, your other kids could be unwinding. They could be playing silently or seeing a relaxing DVD. They can sip some juice and have a treat. When the smallest kid has actually dropped off to sleep to the sound of your voice, put him in the baby crib, and you can even turn on some music, or a recording of you singing or talking gently.

Older Ones' Bath

Both of the older kids can take a bath simultaneously, so long as they get along and do not get too energetic. In case they do get too loud, they ought to shower at different times. In either case, their baths ought to be relaxing. You can speak with them about numerous things, and tell stories, however, they may simply wish to unwind and play.

Bedtime

Lastly, in case you can place both of the older kids to bed simultaneously, that is terrific. Or, in case your partner can place one to bed, that is great. Make certain that you get ample time with each kid. The eldest can go to sleep later on. Tuck the kid in and read a bedtime story, they might wish to talk, so you can still do that. However, let them understand that it's time to sleep in a couple of minutes.

Older Kids

In case you have a big gap in age, you can let the earliest kid aid with the middle kid. Having the kid do something as little as getting the washcloth, or pumping the soap, can make the earliest feel like he is actually required to assist his sibling. It is a terrific means to place some responsibility on his plate. It additionally teaches him about caring.

Chapter 20: SIDS

Sudden Infant Death Syndrome (SIDS) is one that you need to have to understand when it pertains to your infant sleeping. SIDS is a syndrome distinguished by the death of an otherwise healthy infant aged one month to one year. Really little is understood about the reason for SIDS, however, it is deadly. Picture awakening to discover that your stunning infant that was completely great, not ill at all the night prior to had actually, all of a sudden, passed away. You would question if there was something you might have done to stop this relatively quiet killer. SIDS is a scary thing to think about for any brand-new child. Research the syndrome and just follow the guidance of your pediatrician on how to protect against it.

Based upon a study released in the Journal of the American Medical Association, children who pass away from SIDS have irregularities of the brain stem that manages breathing and blood pressure.

Prenatal dangers consist of insufficient prenatal care, nicotine patch, being obese, heroin usage, and infant sex. 61 percent of SIDS deaths are male. Postnatal hazards consist of not breastfeeding, prone sleep position, and excessive bed linen in blankets, clothes, and stuffed animals.

The American Academy of Pediatrics suggests that children sleep on their rears to protect against SIDS. To protect against SIDS, you ought to utilize close-fitting, sheets on a solid mattress, without any excess bed linen. Do not put pillows, packed animals, or fluffy bed linen in the bed. In winter, dress the infant in warm well- fitted clothes.

Sleep Sacks or infant sleeping bags are suggested. The soft bag with holes for the infant's head and arms, in addition to a zipper, permits the bag to be closed around the infant. The protective impacts of the sleeping bag restrict the child's capability to turn from rear to front while sleeping.

SIDS is a really major condition. Throughout your prenatal care, you have to discover as much information as possible about the syndrome, in addition to how to protect against it. Although there might not be a massive quantity of information concerning what triggers SIDS. The important things that are advised against must never ever be put into the infant's crib. Nobody wants your brand-new infant to be among the lives lost to this syndrome, so please follow your physician's directions on precisely what SIDS is and how to protect against it.

I hope that you enjoyed reading through this book and that you have found it useful. If you want to share your thoughts on this book, you can do so by leaving a review on the Amazon page. Have a great rest of the day.

Printed in Great Britain
by Amazon

62102028R00130